THE GOOD, THE BAD, AND THE UGLY
PHILADELPHIA PHILLIES

HEART-POUNDING, JAW-DROPPING, AND GUT-WRENCHING MOMENTS FROM PHILADELPHIA PHILLIES HISTORY

Todd Zolecki

TRIUMPH
B O O K S

Triumph Books and colophon are registered trademarks of Random House, Inc.

Library of Congress Cataloging-in-Publication Data

Zolecki, Todd.
   The good, the bad, and the ugly, Philadelphia Phillies : heart-pounding, jaw-dropping, and gut-wrenching moments from Philadelphia Phillies history / Todd Zolecki.
      p. cm.
   Includes bibliographical references.
   ISBN-13: 978-1-60078-164-3
   ISBN-10: 1-60078-164-0
   1. Philadelphia Phillies (Baseball team)—History. I. Title.
   GV875.P45Z65 2010
   796.357'640974811—dc22

2009049508

This book is available in quantity at special discounts for your group or organization. For further information, contact:

Triumph Books
542 South Dearborn Street
Suite 750
Chicago, Illinois 60605
(312) 939-3330
Fax (312) 663-3557
www.triumphbooks.com

Printed in U.S.A.
ISBN: 978-1-60078-164-3
Design by Patricia Frey
All photos courtesy of Getty Images except where otherwise indicated

To Mom and Dad

CONTENTS

FOREWORD

As a young broadcaster looking for his next big break in baseball, I never really considered the Phillies. Growing up in Texas, I knew plenty about Randall Cunningham, Harold Carmichael, and Reggie White—Philadelphia Eagles and bitter rivals of the Dallas Cowboys. But I didn't know very much about Robin Roberts, Larry Bowa, or Dutch Daulton. I already knew the unmistakable sound of Harry's voice, but as a narrator of my NFL memories. I knew about Michael Jack, of course. I *was* a baseball fan, after all. And I knew about Bull. I remember as a little kid thinking "Luzinski" was a little like "Franzke," at least the way it sounded. I felt some connection to him when I stared at the *Z* in his name on the bubble-gum baseball card.

It was February 2006 when I hopped an early-morning flight from Dallas, destined for Philly. Flying home about 13 hours later, after numerous interviews and introductions, I had a feeling I was destined for Philly, too. Talk about good timing; in the four years since, the Phillies have played 648 regular-season baseball games. Only one of those games was played with the Phillies eliminated from the playoff race! During my first year, the Phillies were mathematically eliminated from the wild-card race after playing game No. 161. Every other game was played either in pursuit of a playoff spot or with a ticket to the postseason already punched. Broadcasters sound better when the team plays well. I know how fortunate I am to have arrived in Philadelphia when I did.

I was at the microphone for Matt Stairs' game-winning home run in Game 5 of the 2008 National League Championship Series, a moment that will forever be remembered by Phillies fans. I was privileged enough to stand on the field—on the pitcher's mound, no less—as the celebration was only just starting after the Phillies won the 2008 World Series over Tampa Bay, watching the fireworks, seeing the faces of the overjoyed players up close, and listening to the roar of more than 45,000 fans rain down from the stands. I stood for hours on the back of a flatbed truck, adorned with bunting and music blaring, as we floated through a see of red along Broad Street. I have experienced things in four short years that many will never get to do, despite a lifetime of hoping.

Of course, appreciating "the good" is made sweeter when you experience—or at least understand—"the bad." To be sure, I appreciate what I've stumbled into: a golden age of Phillies baseball. Three-time NL East champions, back-to-back National League pennants, and a World Series victory in 2008 add up to one of the most impressive eras in the history of this franchise. It has been anchored by some of the best players ever to wear a Phillies uniform.

But this historic era has not been without some bad, too. For many of this generation, there is no worse day in Phillies history than April 13, 2009. Personally, there is no doubt in my mind that it is the worst. One minute, I was standing side-by-side with Harry Kalas, copying down the starting lineups for the game that day in Washington. A few minutes later, standing in the elevator lobby in the basement of Nationals Park, I heard the call for an EMT over the two-way radio held by a ballpark employee. My stomach sank. I don't know how I knew, but I just knew it was HK. Not knowing me or what might be going through my mind at that moment, the employee said aloud, "I'm pretty sure the EMTs aren't even at the ballpark yet." Moments later, I was standing in the television booth, feeling utterly helpless, as Harry lay on the floor struggling to survive.

Sometimes we can enjoy the good when it's happening *because* we've seen so much that's been bad. Sometimes the bad stuff reminds us just how lucky we've been. Riding home on the train that night from Washington, D.C., I thought of a moment just a little more than five months earlier, the moment Harry finally got to call the final out of a World Series championship for the Phillies. I thought of a moment just over four years earlier, the moment I first heard Harry call a Ryan Howard home run as "Outta here" and realized that *I* was the broadcaster in the chair next to one of the great voices in baseball history. Just how lucky we've been, indeed.

I never had to live through the collapse in 1964, the stunning minute-by-minute turnaround on Black Friday, or Joe Carter. I didn't get to experience the euphoria of 1980, the one-of-a-kind characters of '93, or the magic of Whitey Ashburn—be it on the field or behind the microphone. But it's all here in *The Good, The Bad, and the Ugly: Philadelphia Phillies*. Todd Zolecki's collection of stories in this book is a must-have to complete any Phillies library. Lifelong Phillies fans will uncover new artifacts and anecdotes, first-hand accounts from the people who lived the moments you remember so well. Newer fans spoiled by the success of the last few years will perhaps gain a new appreciation and perspective on where this franchise has been, for what it truly means to be a Phillies fan.

Scott Franzke
Philadelphia Phillies
November 2009

P.S. *The ugly?* Try having to look at Larry Andersen at your side every day. There's a reason we're both on the radio.

ACKNOWLEDGMENTS

Nobody said it would be easy writing a baseball book in the middle of the baseball season, especially during the season the Phillies won their first World Series since 1980.

"Are you sure you want to do this?" several people asked.

I was.

At least I thought I was. It was a ton of work and a ton of time. Thankfully, I had a lot of help along the way.

Thanks to Michael Emmerich from Triumph Books. He liked a story I wrote for the *Philadelphia Inquirer* in March 2008 about how Ryan Howard's strikeouts are overrated and asked me if I would be interested in writing this book. If it wasn't for him, I wouldn't have had this experience.

Thanks to the *Inquirer* for giving me the green light to pursue this opportunity.

Phillies vice president of alumni Larry Shenk put me in contact with several former Phillies, including Robin Roberts and Pete Rose. The Baron came through in the clutch. Phillies director of baseball communications Greg Casterioto helped me unearth interesting statistics as I wrote chapters about the Phillies Dream Team.

Current and former Phillies and former opponents like Willie Mays brought new life to stories from the past.

Inquirer baseball writer Jim Salisbury offered plenty of support and taught me just about everything I know about being a baseball writer. I owe him a few Wawa chicken salad hoagies and a bottle of Tom Jenkins BBQ sauce.

Thanks to ESPN.com's Jayson Stark, who was incredibly helpful.

Thanks to everybody who directly or indirectly helped with the research for this book. Phillies historian Rich Westcott has written many excellent Phillies books, which were invaluable resources. The *Inquirer* and *Daily News* archives were huge. The *Inquirer*'s Sam Carchidi helped me reach several former Phillies. Lee Sinins' *Complete Baseball Encyclopedia* helped me put together the Phillies Dream Team. Baseball-Reference.com, every baseball writer's go-to website, and Elias Sports Bureau came up big.

Thanks to John Di Carlo, who took time to read this book before I submitted it.

I also have to thank my family for their support: my parents, Steve and Sue; my brother, Mark (you've...you've earned this); my sister, Betsy; and my sister-in-law, Maryam. They're the best. I'm not sure how a Phillies book will sell in Wisconsin, where I grew up, and Minnesota, where I went to college and have family, but I have a feeling my parents are going to try their best to get this book into as many hands as possible, Phillies fans or not.

I'm OK with that.

I know I have forgotten some important people, but it certainly wasn't intentional. Please forgive me. So to you and everybody else who was nice enough to ask, "Hey, how's the book coming?" Thank you!

THE GOOD

FINALLY!

The buildup had been incredible.

It had been 25 years since Philadelphia's last sports championship and 28 years since the Phillies had won their last World Series. For years fans had imagined where they would be when the drought finally ended.

How would it unfold?

How would it feel once it did?

When would the parade be?

They were about to find out, and they were about to learn it felt a heck of a lot better than they could have imagined. The Phillies had a 4–3 lead over the Tampa Bay Rays in Game 5 of the World Series on October 29, 2008, at Citizens Bank Park. The Rays had the tying run on second base with two outs in the ninth inning, but the Phillies had Brad Lidge on the mound. Lidge hadn't blown a save all year, and he had Rays pinch-hitter Eric Hinske in an 0–2 hole.

Lidge looked to catcher Carlos Ruiz for the sign.

Slider.

Lidge glanced back at Rays pinch-runner Fernando Perez at second base before he threw. The slider tumbled toward home plate with the same nasty bite it had all season. Hinske had no chance. He flailed over the top of it for strike three. Lidge jumped into the air, raised his arms toward the sky, and dropped to his knees.

Ruiz ripped off his mask and ran toward Lidge.

"Oh my God!" Lidge said before Ruiz hugged him in front of the pitcher's mound.

Ryan Howard tackled both of them, and everybody else followed suit as the Phillies quickly formed a pile of red and white.

"I didn't know who I wanted to tackle," Shane Victorino said. "I wanted to tackle every single person. I only could tackle the pile."

The Phillies had won the World Series, and it wasn't a dream. It was real.

There was going to be a parade.

"Champs, baby!" Brett Myers said. "Twenty-eight years!"

The Phillies embarked on their unforgettable journey in February, when they gathered for spring training in Clearwater, Florida. Most prognosticators thought the Phillies, who overcame a seven-game deficit with 17 games to play to win the National League East in 2007, would be good but that the New York Mets would ultimately win the division because they added left-hander Johan Santana in the off-season. Santana's arrival sparked a war of words between the Phillies and Mets when Mets center fielder Carlos Beltran pronounced his team the team to beat.

Beltran should have left the prediction business to Jimmy Rollins, who correctly made that prediction for the Phillies in 2007.

"He's just trying to pull a Jimmy, when you can't have a sequel," Myers said of Beltran. "Sequels are always terrible."

But things looked good for Beltran and the Mets in early September. The Phillies were three and a half games behind them in the NL East and four games behind the Milwaukee Brewers in the NL wild-card race with just 16 games to play. The Phillies had battled adversity just to get to that point, and time was running out. Lidge, Rollins, and Victorino spent time on the disabled list early in the season. Ryan Howard hit just .163 through May 7. Myers, who was the team's Opening Day starter, was optioned to the minor leagues on July 1. Reliever Tom Gordon was lost for the season on July 6. Adam Eaton was optioned to the minors July 29, which was significant only because he was the Phillies' second starting pitcher to go to the minors in less than a month. The offense hit just .237 from June 14 through August 21.

"Last year, we were hot," manager Charlie Manuel said after a 7–3 loss to the Florida Marlins on September 10. "We could score runs, and it seemed like we had enough pitching to get through. We were playing good.... We really got after it. Our team this year, when you're struggling to pitch and score runs, that's tough. But at the same time, I've seen us bounce back. We always have."

They would again. The Phillies swept the Brewers in a four-game series September 11–14 at Citizens Bank Park to pull even with the Brewers in the NL wild-card race and move within a game of the Mets in the NL East. The Phillies finished the season 13–3, the best record in baseball.

The Mets? They finished 7–10 and not only finished three games behind the Phillies in the division, but a game behind the Brewers in the NL wild-card race—missing the playoffs completely. But as good as the Phillies felt to make the postseason in consecutive seasons for the first time since 1980–81, they knew it didn't mean much. The Colorado Rockies swept them in the National League Division Series in 2007. They didn't want a repeat performance.

"I think we were so hell-bent and so focused [on winning] the division last year that we kind of ran out of steam heading into the playoffs," Rollins said. "There's no such thing as pacing yourself, but we know that there is more than just winning the division. We won the division last year, and three games later we were watching with everyone else. We don't want that to happen again, so we'll be a little more under control and hopefully bring home a championship."

Cole Hamels threw eight shutout innings in a 3–1 victory over the Brewers in Game 1 of the NLDS. Victorino hit a memorable grand slam off Brewers ace CC Sabathia in a 5–2 victory in Game 2. The Phillies lost Game 3 at Miller Park 4–1, but in Game 4 Rollins hit a leadoff homer in the first inning and Pat Burrell

FIRST AND FORGOTTEN

The Phillies have played in seven World Series: 1915, 1950, 1980, 1983, 1993, 2008, and 2009.

Five of them are remembered. There are the 1980 and 2008 world championship teams; the 2009 NL championship team; the 1950 Whiz Kids; the 1983 Wheeze Kids; and the dudes with mullets, beer bellies, and bad manners in 1993. Time has erased most of the stories and memories of the 1915 National League champions. Casual Phillies fans would be hard-pressed to name the manager—Pat Moran—or the three Hall of Famers—pitchers Grover Cleveland Alexander and Eppa Rixey and short-stop Dave Bancroft—on the roster.

The Phillies went 88–63 in 1913 to finish in second place, 12½ games behind the New York Giants, but took a step backward in 1914 to finish in sixth at 74–80. Phillies owner William F. Baker fired manager Red Dooin after the season and replaced him with Moran.

"I don't blame Charlie for everything that happened last year," Baker said. "But he lost control of the team, and I think change is advisable and necessary. Fortunately, we didn't have to go far in looking for a successor."

Moran had been a backup catcher in the big leagues for much of his 14-year career with the Boston Beaneaters, Chicago Cubs, and Phillies, where he had been a coach and backup catcher under Dooin. He hit .235 with an unimpressive .283 on-base percentage and .312 slugging percentage, but he loved the game. He studied it. And when he became manager, he knew what he wanted from his players. He stressed fundamentals. He stressed discipline and hard work. He turned spring training into boot camp. Players had to walk a couple miles from the team hotel to the ballpark in St. Petersburg, Florida, where they held camp. Players were reprimanded regularly whenever Moran didn't like what he saw.

"This is not a sixth-place team," Moran said. "This is your bread and butter as well as mine."

But the hard work and two-mile walks did something. The Phillies went 11–1 to start the season. They fell out of first place May 29 but returned to first to stay July 13. They finished 90–62, cruising to the pennant, finishing seven games ahead of the Boston Braves.

"Moran was an inspiring leader," infielder Bobby Byrne said. "He had the knack of building a player up. Pat would make a fellow think he was better than he really was, and first thing you know, the player would be doing better than he knew how."

Alexander needed no such help. He went 31–10 with a 1.22 ERA to lead the pitching staff. Erskine Mayer went 21–15 with a 2.36 ERA. Cravath led the offense. He hit .285 with 24 home runs and 115 RBIs. His 24 homers set baseball's all-time (post-1900) single-season record, which would stand until Babe Ruth hit 29 in 1919.

The Phillies faced the Boston Red Sox in the World Series, a team that had Hall of Famers Ruth, Tris Speaker, Harry Hooper, and Herb Pennock. Alexander allowed eight hits, one run, and two walks in nine innings to beat the Red Sox 3–1 in Game 1 at Baker Bowl. It would be 65 years until the Phillies won another World Series game. The Red Sox scored a run in the top of the ninth to win Game 2 2–1. They scored a run in the bottom of the ninth at Braves Field to win 2–1 in Game 3. They won Game 4 2–1 and Game 5 5–4 to win the Series.

The Phillies came close, but not close enough.

homered twice in a 6–2 victory to win the best-of-five series and put the Phillies into the National League Championship Series for the first time since 1993.

"We don't feel like we should be looking at anything less than a World Series," Rollins said as the Phillies celebrated their NLDS victory at Miller Park. "And that's a World Series win. It's a lot of work. It's not going to be easy, but we weren't geared just to get to the playoffs. We're geared to win. We haven't broken through anything yet. We've just stepped over one hurdle."

The Los Angeles Dodgers were the next hurdle, and the pundits picked them to win the series because they had left fielder Manny Ramirez and manager Joe Torre—and who didn't want to see them in the World Series again?

But Hamels allowed two runs in seven innings, and Chase Utley and Burrell both homered in a 3–2 victory in Game 1. Victorino had four RBIs and Myers had three RBIs in an 8–5 victory in Game 2, which was tempered because Charlie Manuel's mother, June Manuel, died before the game. To add to the heart-break, Victorino learned after the game that his grandmother died in Hawaii. The Phillies traveled to Los Angeles with heavy hearts but remained focused.

"We've got things to do," Manuel said. "I feel like I know my mother would want me in the dugout—because she used to manage a lot for me anyway."

Jamie Moyer got rocked in a 7–2 loss in Game 3 at Dodger Stadium, but even in a shellacking the Phillies showed heart. Benches cleared after Hiroki Kuroda threw over Victorino's head, which was retaliation for Myers throwing behind Ramirez's back in Game 2. The Dodgers had a 5–3 lead in the eighth inning in Game 4 when Victorino hit a game-tying home run into the visitors' bullpen in right field. Matt Stairs followed three batters later and crushed a game-winning two-run home run halfway up the bleachers in right field to win it 7–5.

"You've been here for a month, and you want to get that one big hit where you really feel like you're part of the team," said Stairs, who joined the Phillies after an August 30 trade with the Toronto Blue Jays. "Not that I don't feel like I'm part of the team, but when you get that nice celebration coming in the dugout and you're getting your ass hammered by guys, there's no better feeling than to have that done."

Hamels pitched another gem in a 5–1 victory in Game 5 to clinch the NL pennant, with Nomar Garciaparra fouling out to Ruiz along the third-base line to end the game.

The Phillies were going to the World Series.

"This is going to be the year," Manuel said afterward in the visitors' clubhouse. "I can feel it, yeah."

There certainly was an air of confidence that the Phillies were going to win the World Series, and it started at the top. General manager Pat Gillick loved the scouting reports his top scouts had put together on the Rays. He felt if his players executed, they would win. The Phillies got started early. Utley hit a two-run homer in the first inning, and Hamels allowed two runs in seven innings in a 3–2 victory in Game 1 at Tropicana Field.

The Phillies lost Game 2 4–2 but returned to Philadelphia feeling confident.

They blew a three-run lead in the sixth inning in Game 3, which was delayed an hour and 31 minutes because of rain, but the Phillies loaded the bases with no outs in the ninth inning. Rays manager Joe Maddon added a fifth infielder for Ruiz's at-bat. Ruiz chopped a ball up the third-base line, but Eric Bruntlett beat the throw home to score the winning run in a dramatic 5–4 victory that ended at 1:47 AM.

It wasn't a miracle, but maybe the Phillies had a little help from above. Country star Tim McGraw, son of former Phillies closer Tug McGraw, spread some of his father's ashes on the mound before the game.

"I'm sure he thought it was going to be good luck," Moyer said. "And it turns out that it probably was. It's pretty cool."

"Luck be a lefty," Rollins said with a smile.

The Phillies didn't need much luck in their 10–2 victory in Game 4. Ryan Howard homered twice. Joe Blanton not only pitched well, he also homered.

One more victory.

One more, then a parade.

"Maybe there will be a greater appreciation, if it does happen," Moyer said. "I think sometimes the longer you wait for things, the more you appreciate things. And when you feel like things are earned...I would hate to use the word *assume*, but I feel like our fans are probably the same way. They've given their heart and soul and their hard-earned money to come out here and watch the games. But they've also supported us. And it's exciting because you feel like you're doing this thing together with a city. And I think that's pretty special."

But victory wouldn't come quickly. The Phillies took a 2–0 lead in the first inning in Game 5, which began October 27. But then a cold, hard rain began to fall. It didn't stop, and it got worse as the game continued. It got so bad that most of the infield looked like a pond by the fifth inning. But only after the Rays tied the game 2–2 in the top of the sixth inning did Major League Baseball suspend action for the first time in World Series history.

Cole Hamels throws a pitch against the Tampa Bay Rays during Game 5 of the 2008 World Series on October 27, 2008, at Citizens Bank Park.

Fans were angry. Players were angry. Manuel was angry. This was supposed to be their moment. But not even Mother Nature could stop the Phillies. After a 46-hour delay, play resumed on October 29. Geoff Jenkins, who had been hitless in three postseason at-bats, pinch-hit for Hamels in the bottom of the sixth inning and crushed a leadoff double to right-center field. He eventually scored to give the Phillies a 3–2 lead. The Rays tied the game in the seventh, but Pat Burrell, who had been hitless in 13 World Series at-bats, ripped a leadoff double off the left-center-field wall in the seventh.

"Huge double," Utley said. "Obviously, the biggest double of the year."

Bruntlett, who scored the winning run in Game 3, scored from third on Pedro Feliz's one-out single up the middle to make it 4–3.

"There aren't words to explain it," Feliz said. "I can say it was my best moment in baseball."

J.C. Romero pitched a scoreless eighth. Lidge completed his season of perfection in the ninth.

"We started out in these playoffs saying we were going to put '93 in the past, and we sure did," Myers said. "And we put '80 in the past, too, because our banner is going up there, too."

"It couldn't be sweeter," Burrell said. "It's been a hell of a couple days with the delay and stuff, but to be here now, it's too much. It's too much."

Rollins had predicted the Phillies would win 100 games in 2008. They won 103, including the postseason.

"Golly, this has been a long time coming," he said. "I wanted us to believe that we were good and that we could win. People know it, and they keep it in their heads. They keep it inside. I guess that's the politically correct thing to do, but...if you say something, you better be able to back it up, because people are going to put a target on you. When you have as good a cast as we had last year, and to see the way we picked it up this year, you can say things like that because they're going to back you up. You don't have to go out there, worried and afraid that you're going to be left out there on an island."

The Phillies learned that night that they weren't alone. More than 45,000 fans in the ballpark sang Queen's "We Are the Champions" in perfect harmony. On the streets of Philadelphia, fans celebrated. At homes across the country, Phillies fans jumped up and down and screamed.

From the Team to Beat in 2007 to 100 Wins in 2008, J-Roll had called it all.

What could possibly be next?

"This is just the beginning."

THE LONGEST OUTS

Tug McGraw needed 12 minutes and 54 seconds to finish off the Kansas City Royals in the ninth inning in Game 6 of the 1980 World Series.

That's 774 seconds.

That's nothing.

But it wasn't *nothing*. It was *everything*. The Phillies had waited 97 years for these three outs. They had suffered through World Series losses in 1915 and 1950. They had fallen short in the National League Championship Series in 1976, 1977, and 1978. They had endured one of the worst collapses in baseball history in 1964. They had been close. And when they weren't close, they were far, far away. From 1918 to 1948, the Phillies lost 2,941 games, an astounding 1,111 more games than the New York Yankees and 302 more games than the Boston Braves, the team with the second-most losses in baseball in that 31-year span.

Just 12 minutes and 54 seconds?

Just nothing. It was an eternity.

"It was a long three outs," left fielder Greg Luzinski said. "A long three outs."

The Phillies had a 3–2 lead over the Royals in the best-of-seven series when they entered the ninth inning with a 4–1 lead at Veterans Stadium. Three more outs and they were World Series champions for the first time in franchise history.

McGraw had little left in the tank when he entered the game. He went 5–1 with a 0.52 ERA in 33 appearances down the stretch.

He had thrown eight innings in a tense NLCS against the Houston Astros, and six and two-thirds innings in the World Series, including the eighth inning in Game 6, when he replaced Steve Carlton.

He was gassed.

"He started warming up, and every pitch was high," catcher Bob Boone said. "After a couple of those, it's like, 'What is this?' He and I had a great relationship. He [was] looking at me, and his eyes were like, 'Come on, you know me. What am I doing wrong?' Every pitch was up, up, up. I'm looking at him, now going, 'Is his stride too long? Is his arm up?' I'm looking for all these things. I know I've got to go out there and say something. I'm looking to see what's wrong. Finally, after the second hitter, I was like, 'Well, I've got to go out there.' So I was walking out, and I walked up kind of slow because I wasn't sure what I was going to say.

'Tug?'

'Yeah?' McGraw replied.

'Everything is high.'"

That's it. Boone turned around and walked back to home plate. Boone got to the plate, looked back, and saw McGraw laughing.

"And then he came right back," Boone said.

McGraw had loaded the bases with one out when Frank White stepped into the batter's box. Mercifully for McGraw, White popped up the first pitch into foul territory in front of the Phillies dugout. It looked like a certain out as Boone pursued from behind the plate and Pete Rose pursued from first base.

Boone put his glove out and…the ball popped out! It was going to fall! White and the Royals were going to get a second chance! For a split second, terrible thoughts raced through the minds of millions of Phillies fans. They knew what disasters looked like, and this looked like one of them. But Rose, whom the Phillies signed before the 1979 season as the missing piece to their championship puzzle, wouldn't let that happen. He snatched the ball out of the air for the second out.

"I'm not a good spectator when it comes to playing baseball," Rose said. "The ball was in my area, so I just ran over there. It was a tough play for [Boone] because he was on the dead run at the top step of the dugout. I just saw it pop out of his glove and grabbed it."

MYERS AT THE BAT

Brett Myers can't hit. That's not a knock. That's the truth. He entered Game 2 of the 2008 National League Division Series hitting just .047 (6-for-127) since 2006 to make him the worst hitting pitcher in baseball.

So it would have been forgivable to run to the kitchen when he walked to the plate with a runner on third and two outs in the second inning at Citizens Bank Park. It was Myers vs. Milwaukee Brewers ace CC Sabathia, and Myers had no chance. He swung and missed at the first two pitches to fall behind 0–2. Sabathia threw the next pitch for a ball to make it 1–2. Myers fouled off the fourth pitch. Sabathia threw the fifth pitch into the dirt to make it 2–2. The crowd cheered as Myers fouled off the sixth pitch. It cheered louder as the seventh pitch hit the dirt to make it 3–2.

Sabathia threw a 97-mph fastball, which Myers fouled off again. The crowd roared even louder. Phillies fans seemed to be thinking what everybody else was thinking: *Maybe Myers can make something happen here.* He could, and he did. Sabathia's ninth pitch of the at-bat came inside for a ball. Myers walked. The crowd roared with delight. The moment had shades of 1977, when Phillies fans at Veterans Stadium jeered Dodgers pitcher Burt Hooton so loudly that he came completely unglued and walked four consecutive batters in Game 3 of the NLCS.

"I don't think it frustrated me," Sabathia insisted.

But Sabathia followed his nine-pitch at-bat against Myers to walk Jimmy Rollins on four pitches to load the bases. And four pitchers later, Shane Victorino hit a 1–2 slider over the left-field wall for a grand slam to hand the Phillies a 5–1 lead.

"Did that just really happen?" Victorino asked.

"It was a cutter," Sabathia said. "I threw it in and didn't get it down, didn't bounce it."

Those two at-bats—Myers' walk and Victorino's slam—were two of the most memorable moments in the Phillies' run to the 2008 championship.

"I know I'm a terrible hitter, but I really can't explain it," Myers said. "It was one of those freakish things that I was able to lay off some good pitches to extend his pitch count. Baseball is weird, where you can have a guy that pretty much can't hit a lick go up there and battle a guy that's as good as C.C. I wasn't trying to be a hero in that situation."

He wasn't, but he was. And because he was, Victorino got to be a hero, too.

It remains one of the biggest catches in Phillies history. Of course, Boone and Rose still disagree about why it happened the way it happened. Typically, the catcher handles pop-ups anywhere from the left and right side of home plate and behind. So Boone chased the ball to back up Rose, not to make the catch. Boone expected Rose to call him off, but the farther he ran, the longer he waited to hear Rose's voice.

Where is Pete? Boone thought to himself. *Where is Pete?*

Nothing.

"I'm way out of my area, and I can't hear him," Boone said. "Well, I know I can outrebound him. But I figured I'm going to catch this, he's going to hit me, and we're both going down. It got to the point where it's like, 'Geez, I've got to go for this.' And then I dropped it. And I was so pissed. I was so pissed at Pete, I wanted to kill him. And then all of a sudden his glove came through, he caught the ball, and I wanted to kiss him. But the bottom line is Charlie Hustle, my ass. I'm the one that hustled on that play."

Rose shrugged it off.

"First of all, Boone is probably right when he said that was my ball," he said. "It would have been my ball if it was first and third and one out and I was holding the runner on, you understand what I'm saying? But because the bases were loaded, I was playing way back, like 25 feet off the bag at double-play depth. That made him closer to it than me."

"Oh, bullshit," Boone said. "He was playing deep for a double play? Excuse me? Watch the tape."

Regardless, Rose caught the ball, strutted back toward the mound, and bounced the ball off the artificial turf before flipping it back to McGraw. In a split second, those nightmares turned into the belief that nothing could stop them now.

The Phillies were going to win the World Series.

McGraw needed just one more out, and he and Boone liked their chances against Willie Wilson. Wilson had suffered through a terrible World Series. He was hitting .160 (4-for-25) with 11 strikeouts, a remarkable rate considering he struck out 81 times in 705 at-bats during the regular season. McGraw, his elbow killing him at this point, threw a screwball for a called first strike.

Relief pitcher Tug McGraw celebrates after the final out in Game 6 of the 1980 World Series against the Kansas City Royals at Veterans Stadium on October 21, 1980. Photo courtesy of AP Images.

"We put one screwball in there," Boone said. "Once he got that in his head, he was done."

A couple Philadelphia police officers and their canines trotted behind home plate after the first pitch to Wilson. There already were horses on the field. McGraw saw one of them take a crap on the warning track before he threw the first pitch to Wilson.

"If I don't get out of this inning, that's what I'm going to be in this city," McGraw said. "I'm going to be horseshit."

McGraw's next pitch was a slider, which Wilson fouled off his foot to make it 0–2.

Wilson was a mess.

"Anytime a guy is confused, you throw fastballs," Boone said.

McGraw's first fastball came high for a ball to make it 1–2.

"We let him sit," Boone said. "We were shaking, and he threw a fastball right down the middle. Tug really reached back on that one because he was out of gas."

Wilson swung and missed.

They had won.

McGraw raised his arms in triumph. The Phillies poured out of the dugout and bullpen. The fans in the stands erupted, exorcising 97 years of disappointment and frustration in one joyous roar.

"Everything just sort of froze," shortstop Larry Bowa said. "You reflect back to all the times you came close. All the hardships you went through playing in the minor leagues. All the 0-for-20s. All the people saying you can't do this, you can't do that. It stopped, but all those things went through your mind."

And then he realized he was a World Series champion.

"Let me tell you something," Rose said. "The most awesome sight I've ever seen in sports—and this is Pete Rose talking—was the post–World Series parade. To see a million people in the street on Broad Street and to have 130,000 people waiting for us at JFK Stadium, it was unbelievable. It's a sight I'll never forget. Yeah, that's the greatest thing I've ever seen, and I went through a couple parades in Cincinnati."

Of course it was better. It meant more. The Royals had been in existence 12 years when they played the Phillies in the World

Series. Could their fans really appreciate a World Series championship like Phillies fans could? How could they possibly relate to the heartbreak? *Remember when we lost 93 games as an expansion team in 1969?* Shoot, the Phillies had lost at least 93 games *22 times* by 1980. The New York Yankees had won 22 of their 27 world championships by 1980. What would another championship really mean to them? The Chicago Cubs? They hadn't won a World Series since 1908, although they had been to the World Series seven times since. The Boston Red Sox hadn't won a World Series since 1918, but they had been to the World Series three times since. The Phillies hadn't won a championship since they joined the National League in 1883.

"I think most athletes don't realize the influence they have on a city or a community," pinch-hitting extraordinaire Greg Gross said. "And it's hard because you're caught up in what you're doing. To experience that parade with everybody in the streets and everybody happy, and finishing up at JFK...I guess that's when it sinks in, the kind of effect a winning team can have on a community. Or how much a community puts into supporting a team."

No wonder Rose got goose bumps during the parade.

"Well, you got goose bumps anyway, because it was 35 fucking degrees," he said. "But we didn't care if it was 15 below zero because we were on top of the world."

It was a 97-year wait, with the final 12 minutes, 54 seconds lasting the longest.

STILL CRAZY AFTER ALL THESE YEARS

Philadelphia is known for Ben Franklin and cheesesteaks, not championships and parades (the Mummers notwithstanding).

Entering the 1993 season, the Eagles hadn't won an NFL championship since 1960, the Flyers hadn't won a Stanley Cup since 1975, the Phillies hadn't won a World Series since 1980, and the 76ers hadn't won an NBA championship since 1983.

Philadelphia cherishes its championship teams because championships are hard to come by. It cherishes its teams that simply

THE BOMB

Matt Stairs had been with the Phillies for more than a month in 2008 after an August 30 trade with the Toronto Blue Jays for left-hander Fabio Castro. Stairs, a native Canadian, had always dreamed of a parade down Yonge Street in Toronto, but it would not happen now.

"Now I'll have to learn a new street in Philadelphia and party down there," Stairs said. "Maybe we'll go by [Rocky] Balboa and hang out there."

Stairs hit .294 (5-for-17) with two homers and five RBIs in 16 games for the Phillies down the stretch. He had helped, but he hadn't felt like he had really, truly contributed to the team's success. That changed in Game 4 of the National League Championship Series against the Los Angeles Dodgers at Dodger Stadium. Shane Victorino had just hit a game-tying home run in the top of the eighth inning, and Carlos Ruiz had just hit a two-out single to left field to keep the inning alive.

Dodgers right-hander Jonathan Broxton entered the game with Stairs pinch-hitting for Ryan Madson. Stairs worked Broxton to a 3–1 count, when he crushed Broxton's 95-mph fastball more than halfway up the bleachers in right field for a game-winning two-run home run.

"Charlie [Manuel] always says, 'Throw the head and get it out there,'" Stairs said. "And I got it out there. It was one of those nights where it worked out well against a great pitcher. I just happened to barrel it and— victory."

Stairs' 19 pinch-hit home runs in the regular season rank second in baseball since 1974.

"My whole career, even back in the early days...my approach was [to] try to hit the ball out of the ballpark," he said. "And it's something I enjoyed doing. It carries over from batting practice. In batting practice I try to hit every ball out of the ballpark. And I'm not going to lie, it's fun when you're there and you're hitting balls out of the ballpark. I think the biggest thing is [to] get up there and see how far you're going to hit the ball. I'm not going to lie, I try to hit home runs, and that's it."

Practice paid off. Stairs absolutely crushed that ball. *Destroyed it.*

Stairs had made his contribution.

come close for the same reason. The 1993 Phillies endure as one of the most popular teams in Philadelphia history—not just Phillies history—and they didn't win the World Series.

The '93 Phillies looked like Philly. They acted like Philly. Fans could picture themselves having a beer with them. Some did.

"It was a team that was tailor-made for this city," Mitch Williams said. "We were blue-collar. These people here are blue-collar. They work hard. They work 60-to-80-hour weeks. They respect hard work. And our team worked hard."

"We *were* blue-collar," Milt Thompson echoed. "We just grinded. We went out, we played, we had a great time. We had a lot of fun."

They also won, which was the most important thing. Because crazy, fun personalities aren't quite as lovable if they are losing. The Phillies finished last in the National League East in 1992 at 70–92 but came back to win 97 games in 1993. It made them just the third team since 1900 to go from last place to first place in consecutive seasons.

"They were a very colorful group to watch play," said Bill Giles, who was Phillies president at the time. "Plus, they had a camaraderie. It was amazing how close-knit at least 12 to 15 of them were. They made up their minds in spring training that they were going to win. They'd go out after practice, 12 or 15 of them, have a few pops and talk about what they had to do to win. I went down there in the trainer's room a few times, and they'd be eating fried chicken and drinking beers. They didn't exactly use church language all of the time. It was like your old beer-drinking softball team in your neighborhood."

Nobody believed they could do it. They won their first three games of the season, winning their first season opener since 1984. They were 17–5 in April, a franchise record. They were in first place on May 1 for the first time since 1964. They jumped to a 23–7 start, their best start in franchise history. They were a remarkable 45–17 on June 14 to give them an 11½-game lead in the National League East. They had the best record in baseball and were on pace to win 117 games. That lead shrunk to three games on July 17, but the Phillies got the lead back to 11 games on

August 25. They won the division, despite a late charge from the Montreal Expos.

The Phillies beat the couth and cultured Atlanta Braves in the National League Championship Series to validate the "us vs. them" battle that fueled them to escape the pits of last-place hell.

"All the people who called us rejects; who doubted us; who called us tramps, gypsies, and thieves; who said we were fat and out of shape," Terry Mulholland said. "And I don't care if we changed anyone's mind or not. All I know is that we believed in ourselves, and we proved to the world what we are capable of doing."

The Phillies actually called themselves gypsies, tramps, and thieves. They recognized they had a cast of characters in spring

Philadelphia Phillies pitcher Mitch Williams pitches during the ninth inning of Game 6 of the 1993 World Series against the Toronto Blue Jays at the SkyDome in Toronto. Williams gave up the winning home run to Toronto's Joe Carter as the Jays beat the Phillies 8–6 for their second straight World Series title. Photo courtesy of AP Images.

training with the help of off-season acquisitions like Pete Incaviglia, Danny Jackson, and Larry Andersen. Those newcomers meshed with the likes of John Kruk, Darren Daulton, Lenny Dykstra, Williams, and others to form an eclectic group of personalities.

"This bunch looks like a prison softball team," Williams said in spring training. "But we all get along, and that's very important over the course of a long season."

It is. The most talented teams don't always win. The New York Mets had talented teams in 2007 and 2008 but faded down the stretch. Chemistry matters.

"We never left the clubhouse after a game," Thompson said. "We were in there, talking about the game and figuring out a game plan for the next day. That was unique, even back then. There were teams like that, but not as close-knit as our team was."

It helped them get to the World Series. They had Game 6 in their grasp until Williams threw that unforgettable fastball to Carter, who crushed a game-winning three-run homer in the bottom of the ninth inning. Many players remain convinced they would have won the Series had they won Game 6. Maybe they would have. Maybe not.

But they gave their fans a hell of a ride, and nobody will forget that.

THE WHIZ KIDS

Had Bobby Thomson not hit the "shot heard 'round the world" for the New York Giants in 1951, maybe more people would talk about the dramatic way the Phillies clinched the National League pennant in 1950.

Maybe more people would talk about Richie Ashburn's throw.

Maybe more people would talk about Dick Sisler's home run.

"Hey, we don't care what they say," Robin Roberts said. "Our home run was bigger than Thomson's home run."

There were reasons for that.

CHOOCH'S CHOPPER

The Phillies blew a three-run lead in the sixth inning in Game 3 of the 2008 World Series, but fortunately for them, they had been in tight spots before. Fortunately for them, Tampa Bay Rays left-hander J.P. Howell hit Eric Bruntlett with a pitch to lead off the ninth inning.

That pitch set in motion one of the craziest and most dramatic innings in Phillies history.

Rays right-hander Grant Balfour replaced Howell, and he uncorked a wild pitch to send Bruntlett to second. The ball hit so hard off the backstop and rebounded back to catcher Dioner Navarro so quickly that Navarro tried to throw out Bruntlett at second. But the throw scooted into the outfield, which allowed Bruntlett to reach third.

Balfour intentionally walked Shane Victorino and Greg Dobbs to load the bases with nobody out. Rays manager Joe Maddon then had right fielder Ben Zobrist move into the infield to give the Rays five infielders for Carlos Ruiz's at-bat. Ruiz chopped a ball down the third-base line, and Bruntlett ran hard as third baseman Evan Longoria picked up the ball and desperately tried to flip it home. The ball sailed over Bruntlett's head as he slid home safely to win the game 5–4.

"I saw the ball go into the ground," Bruntlett said. "I knew it wasn't hit very hard, so I knew I just had to high-tail it and go as hard as I could.... It was one of those deals where it kind of felt like everything was in slow motion. I felt like I should have been moving faster, and I couldn't, because I wanted to get there so quickly. It felt like a long 90 feet at that point."

The game, which had an hour-and-31-minute rain delay, ended at 1:47 AM. It was a long night, but it was worth it.

First, the Phillies hadn't been to the World Series since 1915. The Giants had been to eight World Series since 1915. They won three of them. Second, the Phillies almost blew it. They had held a comfortable seven-and-a-half-game lead over the Boston Braves and Brooklyn Dodgers with just 11 games to play, but they lost eight of their next 10 to turn that once comfortable lead into a perilously thin one-game lead over the Dodgers entering the final game of the season.

The collapse had little to do with being too tight. They had lost Curt Simmons, who went 17–8 with a 3.40 ERA, to the National Guard on September 10. They lost Bubba Church, who went 8–6 with a 2.73 ERA, on September 15, when Cincinnati Reds first baseman Ted Kluszewski hit him in the face with a line drive. Bob Miller, who went 11–6 with a 3.57 ERA, had to be pulled from a start September 16 because of a sore shoulder.

They lost three starters in a span of seven days.

They had other injuries, too. Sisler had been fighting a sore left wrist for some time. Catcher Andy Seminick broke his ankle on a play at the plate September 27 but somehow continued to play. Bill Nicholson missed the final few weeks of the season because of diabetes.

But the injuries couldn't change the fact that the Phillies needed to beat the Dodgers at Ebbets Field in their October 1 season finale to clinch the pennant. If they lost, they would have to play a three-game playoff against the Dodgers, with Games 1 and 2 at Ebbets Field and Game 3, if necessary, at Shibe Park.

"The last three weeks of September were a shame because that wasn't anything like the ballclub we had been," Roberts said.

The Phillies were up against it, so manager Eddie Sawyer went with his ace. He told Roberts about an hour before the franchise's biggest game in 35 years that he would start on just two days' rest, his fourth start in nine days. Roberts figured he might pitch, so he wasn't surprised.

The Phillies took a 1–0 lead in the top of the sixth, but Pee Wee Reese hit a fluke inside-the-park home run in the bottom of the sixth to tie the game when the ball came to rest at the top of a ledge in right field. The score remained tied as Roberts dragged his tired body to the mound in the bottom of the ninth. He walked Cal Abrams to start the inning, and Reese ripped a single to left to put runners on first and second with no outs. Duke Snider stepped up and lined Roberts' first pitch up the middle for a hit. Abrams hesitated briefly at second, but Dodgers third-base

DOUBLE TROUBLE

The Phillies returned to Citizens Bank Park for Game 5 of the 2008 World Series on October 29 with people wondering if they had lost momentum. The Rays had tied the game in the top of the sixth inning before Major League Baseball suspended play October 27 because of rain and unplayable conditions. Cole Hamels was finished pitching, and the Phillies seemed rattled by the way things had unfolded. But all that speculation—how would this affect the Phillies?—ended when Geoff Jenkins ripped a leadoff double to right-center field in the bottom of the sixth. He scored to give the Phillies a 3–2 lead.

Matt Stairs had his moment to shine in Game 4 of the NLCS, when he hit a game-winning two-run home run. Jenkins, who had been hitless in three postseason at-bats and who hadn't had a hit since the final day of the regular season on September 28, just had his moment in Game 5 of the World Series.

"We were talking about that after the inning," Jenkins said. "He said, 'Hey, now you know what I'm talking about.' To be able to pitch in, get a big hit, and score a run, it's one of those things I won't forget for the rest of my life."

The Rays tied the game in the top of the seventh, but Pat Burrell, who was 0-for-13 in the World Series, crushed a leadoff double off the left-center-field wall in the bottom of the inning. It led to pinch-runner Eric Bruntlett scoring the winning run on a single from Pedro Feliz. Burrell, who entered the off-season a free agent, celebrated that night knowing that it could have been his last at-bat in a Phillies uniform.

"It is emotional," Burrell said. "But I'm going to enjoy it."

coach Milt Stock waved Abrams home. He figured that Ashburn, who wasn't known for his arm in center field, had no chance to throw out Abrams at the plate.

He figured wrong. Ashburn made a perfect throw to catcher Stan Lopata, and Abrams was out by several feet.

"Richie didn't have the worst arm, but he didn't have an arm like Willie Mays, either," Lopata said. "But I'll tell you one thing.

That throw was the greatest throw I've ever seen. I don't care what anybody says. Whitey threw a perfect strike to me."

Call it the Greatest Throw in Phillies History.

"People didn't respect Richie's arm," Roberts said. "He didn't have a strong arm, but he had an accurate arm. So he had a chance to throw out people during the year because they would run on him. The third-base coach thought it was Richie, and they always ran on him, but they didn't realize that the ball had been a line drive and Abrams had held up a little bit. It was a perfect throw. If he had stopped at third, they would have had the bases loaded with Jackie Robinson up and no outs."

But the Dodgers still had runners on second and third with one out, Robinson at the plate, Carl Furillo on deck, and Gil Hodges in the hole.

Sawyer visited Roberts on the mound.

"Put Robinson on and keep the ball down on Furillo," he said.

That's all he said. Sawyer turned around and returned to the dugout. Roberts followed his first order. He intentionally walked Robinson, who hit .328 with 14 homers and 81 RBIs, to load the bases with one out to bring up Furillo, who hit .305 with 18 homers and 106 RBIs. But Roberts threw a fastball up in the zone to Furillo. Fortunately for Roberts, Furillo popped out in foul territory to first baseman Eddie Waitkus for the second out.

Could Roberts actually work out of this jam?

He still had to get through Hodges, who hit .283 with 32 homers and 113 RBIs. Hodges hit a 1–0 pitch to right field. It should have been an easy play for right fielder Del Ennis, but he battled the sun and caught the ball against his body to end the inning. Legend has it that Ennis had the stitching of the baseball imprinted on his chest because the ball hit him so hard, but Roberts acknowledged that "might be a story that got a little better as we went along."

Stitches on his chest or not, Ennis caught it and Roberts worked out of an inning that had runners on first and second with no outs and bases loaded with one out.

"It was a miracle and a relief combined," Roberts said.

Now they just had to score. Roberts and Waitkus hit back-to-back singles to start the tenth. Ashburn followed and bunted a ball up the third-base line, but Dodgers pitcher Don Newcombe made a nice play to throw out Roberts at third for the first out. That set up Sisler's heroics. He fell behind 0–2 before he smacked a 1–2 fastball up and away over the left-field fence for a three-run homer to hand the Phillies a 4–1 lead.

"My wrist was bothering me," Sisler said. "I took a shot before the game, but it was still sore. If Newcombe had come inside with his fastball, he probably would've knocked the bat out of my hands. But he didn't. He threw me a fastball high and away. I still don't know why he did it. That's a pitch I could always handle. I went with it and hit it good."

Teammates mobbed Sisler as he touched home plate, feeling equal parts excitement and relief.

"Everybody is just hanging in there. It had been such a long stretch," Roberts explained. "He hit a line drive. Left center was pretty close at Ebbets Field. It was about 345 to the fence. You knew he hit it good, but you didn't know whether or not it was going to carry out of the park. We couldn't tell. By golly, it went in the first or second row. That home run was one of the all-timers. They talk about big hits in baseball, well, certain guys have certain big hits, and that was the biggest I was ever involved with."

"To us, that was *the* home run," Lopata said.

Roberts felt energized as he walked to the mound for the bottom of the tenth. So much so that he retired Roy Campanella and pinch-hitters Jim Russell and Tommy Brown in order to end the game and begin the celebration.

"Fortunately we were able to win the last day," Roberts said. "Ashburn threw the guy out at home. Sisler hit the home run. The way we went to it, it was a great relief that we were able to pull it off, because we had almost blown a big lead. That would have been terrible to live with."

The Phillies reached the World Series for the first time since 1915, but the New York Yankees swept them in four games.

The sweep never took the luster off the Whiz Kids.

The National League champion Philadelphia Phillies, the Whiz Kids, pose in Connie Mack Stadium in 1950. Hall of Famer Robin Roberts is standing, far left, and Richie Ashburn is seated in the front row, center.

"It's kind of hard to explain," Roberts said of the Whiz Kids' enduring popularity. "In '48 we almost finished in last place, but in the tail end of the '49 season we really started getting it together. We came in third that year. There was just a feeling that things were working. We were awful young in '48. Then [Granny] Hamner, Ashburn, Puddin' Head [Jones], they all just started playing big-league baseball. It was just one of those things. It was a perfect fit. It all came together at the right time."

"We won," Simmons said, offering his take on the Whiz Kids' appeal. "The Dodgers used to win all the time. I don't think we were favorites. We snuck in at the end. I was gone, guys were hurt, and Robbie pitched every other day it seemed like. We hadn't won in so long. That's why it was special."

And they won with one of the greatest games in baseball history. Maybe even better than "the shot heard 'round the world."

"I don't care what they say about Bobby Thomson's home run," Lopata said. "I don't care what they say about all the great hits and great series that have happened since. They can't take that away from us."

Nobody would.

THE WHEEZE KIDS

The Phillies were in first place in the National League East on July 17, 1983.

They fired their manager the next day.

It is the first and only time in baseball history that a first-place team has fired its manager in season. But the Phillies whacked Pat Corrales because they felt their roster of aging stars—better known as "the Wheeze Kids"—had underachieved. The Phillies were 43–42 with a core that included Mike Schmidt, Steve Carlton, Pete Rose, Joe Morgan, and Tony Perez, and their underachievement hadn't sat well with Phillies president Bill Giles and general manager Paul Owens, who said before the season this was the finest team they had ever assembled.

So Owens fired Corrales and moved himself into the dugout.

"We feel the team is not performing as well as we anticipated and that Paul is the man to make it play to the expectations we had," Giles said during a July 18 news conference at Veterans Stadium. "Yes, we are in first place, but a 43–42 record is not what we had expected to be doing."

The move surprised many, both inside and outside the organization.

"Somehow it seems fitting that the franchise with the longest sustained history of failure would pick its centennial season to cashier a manager who was doing a creditable job and replace him with a 59-year-old front-office executive who had managed only 80 games (33–47) in the last quarter of a century," wrote the *Washington Post*'s Thomas Boswell.

THE BOND THEY SHARE

There aren't many Whiz Kids left.

There is Robin Roberts and Curt Simmons, Bob Miller and Stan Lopata, Jackie Mayo and Putsy Caballero. Paul Stuffel, who made three appearances for the Phillies in 1950, and Maje McDonnell, who coached, remain.

The rest are gone.

"I was here by myself last night wishing how I could just sit around and have a beer with Puddin' Head [Jones] and [Granny] Hamner and Del [Ennis] and Bill Nicholson and my buddy [Eddie] Waitkus," the 82-year-old Miller said from his Michigan home in 2008. "Boy, it's hard to believe they're all gone, because I close my eyes and we're all young again."

Miller closes his eyes and pictures himself in the corner of the Phillies clubhouse at Shibe Park, having drinks with his buddies and talking about their latest victory. He keeps his eyes closed and sees his teammates playing cards on the train. He sees his friends at dinner, enjoying a nice steak. But most of all he hears the laughter and the voices and the stories from almost 60 years ago.

"Puddin' Head was quite a guy," Miller said of Jones, who spoke with a thick Southern accent. "They used to call me Booger. He'd say, 'Booga, keep the ball down because my footses is hurting today. My footses really hurts, Booga.' We all sat together in the corner of the clubhouse. It was Waitkus, Puddin' Head, and Maje McDonnell and myself. And after the game we'd have our beers together and hash over the ballgame and stuff. I just loved listening to Willie talk with that Southern drawl. Man, he was beautiful. He wouldn't hurt a soul. I loved those guys. Man, they were great. They really were great."

Miller remembers the times he brought his father, a proud Detroit police officer, into the clubhouse after games. McDonnell and Dick Sisler used to love to joke with Miller's dad.

"Hey, Sisler, does your old man work?" McDonnell said, loud enough for Miller's father to hear.

"No, Maje, he's a cop," Sisler always replied.

"And God almighty, my old man broke up when they used to do that," Miller said, laughing. "Every time they saw my dad, they'd say the same damn thing, and he found it really funny. He got a kick out of that."

The bond among the Whiz Kids, both dead and living, remains strong. Miller described that bond when he recalled how he ran into Andy Seminick in Florida many years ago while Seminick was working as an instructor for the Phillies.

"There was old '21' in a uniform with a fungo bat and his legs crossed working with the Phillies' young kids," Miller said. "And I yelled, 'Hey, Wasil!' That's what we used to call him because that was his middle name. And he turned around and said, 'Booger!' And now here's two old guys in their seventies running at each other and embracing and hugging. Now that's love. I mean, that is appreciation of being together and being a part of something that was fantastic."

And that will never die.

"I don't know what happened," Perez said. "We were in first place at the time. It was close, but we were in first."

Corrales thought some of the aging stars appeared unmotivated. Owens partially agreed, but he felt the manager should be able to motivate them.

"It was tough to let Pat go, but we had to do something," Owens said. "There were big clubhouse problems with that team, and they had to be fixed. That one time at least, the repairs took."

Owens didn't turn around the Phillies' fortunes immediately. They lost five of their first seven games but went 18–7 in the following 25 games to improve to 63–54 on August 18. They followed that stretch with a 6–13 skid to fall to 69–67, which put them into a third-place tie September 5.

Then they took off. Morgan had struggled most of the season but carried the team in the final three weeks. He was hitting just .204 on September 9 but hit .369 with three home runs and 13 RBIs in his final 17 games. The Phillies won 21 of their remaining 26 games, including an 11-game winning streak, to clinch the division on September 28 with three games to play.

"We had a great September," Perez said.

"Nobody had really good years, but when it came to that last month, we kind of showed what veterans are all about," said Gary Matthews, who won National League Championship Series MVP honors against the Los Angeles Dodgers. "We took them to task and we ended up winning it without guys having super years."

He was right. The Phillies hit just .249 as a team. They had eight players with 300 or more at-bats, but none of them hit better than .275. Somehow they finished third in the league in runs scored as they benefited from the second-best pitching staff in the National League with a 3.35 ERA. John Denny went 19–6 with a 2.37 ERA to win the Cy Young Award. Al Holland saved 25 games. Holland, Willie Hernandez, and Ron Reed formed a formidable trio in the bullpen.

Did the midseason firing help?

"They were running it over there in Philadelphia," Matthews said of veteran players like Rose, Morgan, Perez, Schmidt, and Carlton. "They had somebody in charge of the ship, but they were the real ones running it. Ain't no doubt in my mind."

The Phillies beat the Dodgers 3–1 in the best-of-five NLCS to advance to their second World Series in four years. But after the Phillies beat the Baltimore Orioles 2–1 in Game 1, the Orioles won the next four to win the championship.

The Phillies had six players on their Opening Day roster who were 38 or older: Carlton (38), Tug McGraw (38), Morgan (39), Reed (40), Perez (41), and Rose (42).

"We got a kick out of it," Perez chuckled. "We knew we were old, and we knew we were at the end of our careers. So we just enjoyed playing with a team that won the National League pennant. It was fun. It was a good memory."

THE BAD

GAME 6

Joe Freakin' Carter.

Mitch Williams hears that name every day. When people see him, they *have* to ask him about October 23, 1993. The pitch. The swing. The moment. They have to ask, even though they know the answer. They have heard the answer a million times, just like he has heard the question a million times. Maybe they ask him because they think he will tell them something that he has never told another soul. But in reality, they ask because they want to hear it for themselves.

"Fastball, down and in," Williams will say. "Wanted it up and away."

We know Carter hit his fastball over the left-field wall at SkyDome for a three-run home run to give the Toronto Blue Jays an 8–6 victory over the Phillies in Game 6 of the 1993 World Series. It clinched Toronto's second consecutive World Series championship.

We know that. We have seen the replay. But we still want to know why. So Williams answers again and again.

"I just get it out of the way," he said. "I get the question every day, so I just go ahead and clear it up so we can get to whatever it is that we need to talk about. They know I'm not going to make an excuse for it. It was a mistake. I made it, and that's all there is to it. But Joe Carter comes up in some fashion every day. What do you do with it? What are you going to do? Hey, if I would have gotten him out, nobody would know who the hell I am."

Williams kept things interesting for the Phillies in '93. He saved 43 games but had fans walk the high wire with him on more than a few occasions. He took the loss in Game 4 of the World Series, when the Phillies turned a 14–9 lead in the seventh inning into a 15–14 loss to give the Blue Jays a 3–1 lead in the best-of-seven series. Death threats followed Game 4, and while Williams never has offered them as an excuse for his performance in Game 6, his father said that Williams hardly slept.

Fans still wonder what would have happened had Phillies manager Jim Fregosi allowed Roger Mason to finish the eighth inning in Game 6. Mason had thrown two and a third scoreless innings when Fregosi walked to the mound to replace him with David West with one out. Mason had thrown just 27 pitches and had retired the last seven batters he faced, but he also hadn't been terribly effective when he had been extended during the regular season. Regardless, West entered and walked John Olerud on five pitches. Fregosi immediately replaced West with Larry Andersen, who was out of gas. He loaded the bases before he got Pat Borders to pop out to end the inning.

It proved important. Instead of Williams facing the bottom of the Blue Jays' order in the ninth—Tony Fernandez, Ed Sprague, and Borders—he had to face Rickey Henderson, Devon White, Paul Molitor, and Carter.

"I think I could have gone longer," Mason said. "But Jim's used the bullpen the same way all year. You get that late in the game and have a hitter like Olerud coming up, you're going to go with your left-hander."

Turning over the lineup boosted the Blue Jays' confidence.

"We were hoping for Mitch to come in," Henderson said. "We know he has a tendency to be a little wild. We were hoping he would walk a couple guys and then throw one over. And he did."

Williams walked Henderson to lead off the inning. He got White to fly out to left field for the first out, but Molitor singled to center to put the tying run on second base with Carter at the plate.

Pitcher Mitch Williams walks off the field as Joe Carter (No. 29) of the Toronto Blue Jays dances his way around the bases after hitting the Series-winning home run in Game 6 of the 1993 World Series at the SkyDome on October 23, 1993, in Toronto.

First pitch: ball one. Second pitch: ball two. Williams got Carter to take his third pitch for a called strike. He got Carter to swing and miss at his fourth pitch to even the count at 2–2. Phillies catcher Darren Daulton put out his mitt and gave Williams the sign. Williams shook off Daulton, who put down the sign again. The shakeoff was a decoy. They were going with a fastball.

Williams slide-stepped as he threw. He had never used a slide-step in his career until the playoffs, but he incorporated it because he respected the speed the Atlanta Braves had in the National League Championship Series and the Blue Jays had in the World Series. Maybe Williams would have made a better pitch if he had skipped the slide-step and gone with his normal delivery. Nobody will know, because Williams threw the fastball down and in, and Carter crushed it.

Gone.

That pitch and that moment remains burned into the memories of millions of Phillies fans. Williams knows this. He is reminded every day. But despite those memories, Williams remains in Philadelphia, where he is admired. The Phillies asked him to throw out the first pitch before Game 1 of the 2008 National League Division Series against the Milwaukee Brewers. He played up his "Wild Thing" image and purposely threw the ball about 20 feet over the head of catcher Lou Marson and against the backstop.

Fans roared with approval.

From love to hate to love again.

"I think it's honesty," Williams said. "You don't make excuses in this city. I never did. I've come back here, and they've been great. I couldn't ask to be treated any better than they treat me here."

BLACK FRIDAY

Jerry Martin knew the situations when he would replace Greg Luzinski in left field, and because this was one of those situations, he had started to warm up.

Martin, a reserve outfielder, had begun to run up and down the ramp between the Phillies dugout and clubhouse at Veterans

Stadium, which had been his routine throughout the 1977 season. He had started to run because he knew—he absolutely knew—he would be in left field to start the ninth inning on October 7 in Game 3 of the National League Championship Series. The Phillies, who went 101–61 that year, appeared primed to reach their first World Series since 1950, and there seemed no way Phillies manager Danny Ozark would leave anything to chance. If the Phillies won Game 3 to take a 2–1 series lead, they had the next two games at the Vet—a tremendous advantage for a team that went 60–21 at home during the season.

This might have been the best team in Phillies history. The Phillies won 101 games in 1976, getting swept in the NLCS by the Cincinnati Reds. But the '77 Phillies believed this was their year. They had Mike Schmidt and Steve Carlton, Luzinski and Larry Bowa, Larry Christenson and Bake McBride, Gene Garber and Tug McGraw. They were loaded, and they were just three outs away from putting a choke hold on the series.

Martin finished loosening up on the ramp. He returned to the dugout and noticed Luzinski sitting on the bench.

"You're going in, right?" Luzinski hollered.

"Yeah, I'm going in," Martin replied.

He was going in. He always went in. But Martin kept looking down at Phillies bench coach Bobby Wine for the signal. He kept looking and looking. He kept waiting and waiting.

"I'm going in, right?"

"I don't know yet," Wine replied.

Ozark decided to stick with Luzinski, despite the fact that Martin had replaced him in left field 41 times during the regular season.

"I said, 'Well, that's no big deal,'" Martin said. "We still had a two-run lead. No big deal. No big deal."

"The percentages of the ball being hit at you are pretty slim," Luzinski said.

The 63,719 fans rocked the Vet as Garber retired Dusty Baker and Rick Monday for the first two outs in the ninth. The crowd had been impressively loud from the jump. They booed Dodgers starter Burt Hooton so badly that he unraveled and walked four consecutive batters in the bottom of the second inning as the Phillies took a 3–2 lead.

"It was a packed house, and the people were screaming and chanting, 'Geno, Geno, Geno,'" Garber said. "Everybody who plays would dream about that situation. There were two outs."

Then all hell broke loose.

Dodgers pinch-hitter Vic Davalillo bunted for an infield single to keep the inning alive. Pinch-hitter Manny Mota followed. He had appeared in 49 games for the Dodgers and pinch-hit in 48 of them, hitting a remarkable .395. He smacked a two-strike pitch to deep left field. Luzinski took a couple steps in at the crack of the bat, then broke back on the ball. Luzinski leaped near the wall but couldn't make the catch. Davalillo scored to make it 5–4, and Mota cruised to third as Luzinski's throw got away from second baseman Ted Sizemore.

"Would I have caught the ball?" Martin said. "I'm 99.9 percent sure I would have caught that ball. You never know. Maybe I would have dropped it. But the chances are I would have caught that ball. I wouldn't have even hit the wall. Bull broke in a couple steps, then went back. Who knows? Eight or nine times out of 10 he'll probably catch that ball. It's just one of those deals."

Luzinski is certain he would have caught the ball, but he thought they weren't positioned properly in the outfield.

"I think we should have been playing deeper to begin with, in a no-doubles situation, that type of thing," he said. "We were in a little closer than we needed to be, but there are no excuses. I still say the ball never hit the wall. It hit the top of my glove and went straight up. And I caught it. Then the throw came into Sizemore. Now, I don't know what he was doing, but the ball got by him. If it doesn't get by him, it's a whole different situation."

Ozark said afterward that he kept Luzinski in left field because he wanted his bat in the lineup in case the Dodgers tied the game or took the lead. It turned out to be his worst decision with the Phillies.

Davey Lopes followed Mota and smoked a ball that deflected off third baseman Mike Schmidt's glove, but the ball took a fortuitous bounce into Larry Bowa's bare hand. He fired a missile to first base,

Outfielder Greg Luzinski prepares to bat against the Pittsburgh Pirates at Three Rivers Stadium in September 1977 in Pittsburgh, Pennsylvania.

but first-base umpire Bruce Froemming ruled Lopes safe as Mota scored to tie the game.

"To this day, if you look at the replay, he's out," Bowa said.

If he'd been called out, the game would have been over with the Phillies up 2–1.

"I can still see the play," Froemming said. "It was a photo finish. Lopes and the ball arrived at the same time. All I know is that [National League official] Fred Fleig and the Phillies' brass looked at replays 12, 14 times in the trailer the next day, and Fred told me they couldn't call it. I had one shot at it, and he was safe. I got it right."

Lopes agreed.

"I was safe," he said.

You won't find one player on the Phillies who agrees with Froemming or Lopes. In fact, Martin said he will go to the grave believing Lopes was out and the game should have been over.

"He made a hell of a play," Martin said of Bowa. "That ball was smoked. He smoked that ball. Schmidt's got his glove on it, the ball bounced off him, Bo bare-handed it, and I still say he was out. I bet if they went back and got it and super-slomo'd it down, I guarantee it's 99.9 percent sure he's out. That's my feeling. Of course, I'm the one on the losing end of that damn thing. It would be interesting to really see that thing slowed down to the point where you actually see the ball hit [first baseman Richie] Hebner's mitt and see where his foot is. I think it's going to be in the air. That's my thinking."

The madness continued from there. A Garber pickoff attempt deflected off Lopes and Lopes scampered to second. He scored on Bill Russell's single up the middle to hand the Dodgers an improbable 6–5 lead.

"It went right through my legs," Garber said. "It was one thing after another. There were five things that happened in that inning that just wouldn't happen again. It went from being the most fun I've ever had pitching in my whole life...to a nightmare. All in a few pitches. I didn't sleep at all that night."

The Phillies lost Game 4 4–1 in a miserable downpour, to lose the series.

The greatest team in Phillies history suddenly wasn't.

"You always think you're better than the team that beat you, and then when you sit back and let a week go by, you start thinking differently," Bowa said. "But that year was different. I really thought we were better than the Dodgers that year, and we just didn't get the breaks."

Martin wonders *What if?* What if he had been in left? What if he had caught the ball? Where would the Phillies have gone from there?

"One thing I remember about that night is they went ahead, and in the bottom of the ninth we went quietly," he said. "And for the 60,000 people that were in the stands, it was eerie quiet. It was very quiet. It seemed like it happened so damn fast. Damn, what happened there? And then when we got three outs real quick it was just like, you know, *damn.*"

It was Black Friday.

Martin is still asked about Black Friday. Early in the 2008 season, as he filled in for Lopes as the Phillies' first-base coach, he brought a ball to a child down the first-base line at Citizens Bank Park. He was handing the ball to the child when the man next to him asked, "Hey, why didn't they put you in?"

"I swear," Martin said. "I said, 'Do you know how many times I've heard that?' In the annals of Philadelphia baseball history, I'm probably known more for the game I was not in than any of the stuff that I did on the field the whole time I was there. That's the damn truth. It is the way it is, though. I did do a few good things on the field while I was there, but nobody remembers that. They remember the game I was not in. It was a tough situation. It was hard to swallow."

And impossible to forget.

NO! NO! NO! NO! NO!

Ruben Amaro ran into Chico Ruiz a few times after he stole home plate to help break the hearts of millions of Phillies fans in 1964. Their conversations frequently returned to that one play.

"The reason that you stole home plate is because you were not in the ballgame," Amaro said. "You probably didn't even know that Frank Robinson was hitting."

Ruiz just shrugged and said he really didn't know why he stole home. He just stole.

The Phillies had a six-and-a-half-game lead in the National League with 12 games to play September 21, 1964, when they opened a three-game series against the Cincinnati Reds at Connie Mack Stadium. It was the top of the sixth inning in a scoreless tie when Ruiz hit a one-out single to right field. Vada Pinson also singled but was thrown out at second as Ruiz scooted to third.

That's when Robinson stepped into the batter's box.

That's when Ruiz broke for home.

"No! No! No! No! No!" Reds third-base coach Reggie Otero shouted at Ruiz.

But it was too late. Ruiz couldn't be stopped. He was stealing home plate with a Hall of Famer in the batter's box.

"If I'd had a gun, I would have shot him," Dick Sisler, the Reds' interim manager, said.

"Nobody is that frickin' dumb," Amaro said.

Phillies right-hander Art Mahaffey couldn't have been more startled to see Ruiz running. He only needed to throw the ball near the plate and Ruiz would have been out by 10 feet, but instead he threw wildly and Ruiz scored easily. The Reds won 1–0 to start the Phillies' 10-game losing streak that cost them the pennant in the worst collapse in baseball history.

That play is not the reason why the Phillies lost 10 straight. They didn't leave the ballpark that night with an imminent sense of doom. But it is the moment that everybody remembers as the beginning of a terrible end.

"It was like Ted Williams hitting," Mahaffey said. "Frank Robinson, Willie Mays, Henry Aaron, you're concentrating on the hitter. And this rookie steals home. Totally unbelievable. It was just so stupid."

"It never should have happened," Phillies catcher Clay Dalrymple said. "All he had to do was deliver the ball to me, and instead he throws the ball 10 feet to my right. He panicked. I don't know why he panicked when he saw Ruiz coming down the line, but boy he did. He panicked big time. There was no way to catch it. No way. I don't know what the hell went through his head. You don't throw the ball outside, you throw inside so you can knock Frank down, so I can put the tag on the runner coming in. You brush him back. God only knows what was going through his mind."

Dalrymple said pitchers are programmed to do certain jobs certain ways. And any variance from those mechanics—the way they stand on the rubber, the way they throw to first, the way they cover first base—they will mess up nine times out of 10. Mahaffey wasn't programmed to throw a ball to the plate when a knucklehead steals home with a Hall of Famer in the batter's box.

"Mahaffey gets pissed off at me when I mention this because I'm knocking him, but he's no different from any other pitcher I've ever seen," Dalrymple said.

Had Ruiz been thrown out at the plate, Sisler said he might as well have continued running to San Diego—Cincinnati's Triple A team. Otero said that Ruiz could have continued running (and eventually swimming) to Cuba—his homeland. But Ruiz made it, so he stuck around.

Ruiz had an undistinguished career in eight seasons with Cincinnati and California. He never had more than the 311 at-bats he had as a rookie in 1964. He hit just two home runs in his career, both of them in '64. He had a career-high 16 RBIs in '64. He was a career .244 hitter. But he is immortal in Philadelphia. Ruiz, who died in an automobile accident on February 9, 1972, is remembered because of one play. Had he never stolen home to start the Phillies on their infamous collapse, he would have been just another Onix Concepcion, Pedro Gonzalez, or John Donaldson—players with similar careers statistically as Ruiz. But in Philadelphia, Ruiz is a name that stirs heartbreak. Fans who lived through 1964 know the name well. But even younger fans, casual fans, have heard of Chico Ruiz. They might not know exactly who he is or what he did, but they know his name has dark connotations. Chico Ruiz signifies catastrophe. And that's why, more than 40 years later, the play still stirs emotions for those who lived through it.

"You've got the best hitter in the clutch in the National League hitting with two strikes, and all of a sudden this guy wants to steal home plate," Amaro said. "You know, the tragedy of this situation is that if it would have been a ball around the plate, Frank was going to swing. If it would have been a ball that the catcher could have caught and Frank would have missed, it would have been three outs and it didn't matter. If it would have been a ball, he would have been out by 20 feet."

But instead of a ball, Mahaffey threw an uncatchable ball.

"We were pretty dumbfounded by what was happening," Amaro said. "It was the beginning of a lot of things. I don't think that it's something that triggered anything. We just kept making mistakes."

But that one mistake stands out among the rest.

THE UGLY

THE DARK AGES

The frustration. The angst. The cynicism. It had to start somewhere.

But when? The Phillies joined the National League in 1883 and were pretty respectable in their first 35 years. They reached the World Series in 1915. They had 22 winning seasons. They finished in the first division 21 times. They had Hall of Fame talents like Ed Delahanty, Billy Hamilton, and Grover Cleveland Alexander. They were talented, competitive, and competent.

It all changed December 11, 1917, when Phillies owner William Baker traded Alexander to the Chicago Cubs for a couple of stiffs and $60,000. The trade triggered a 31-year run of horrific baseball. From 1918 through 1948, the Phillies went 1,752–2,941 for a laughable .373 winning percentage. To put that into perspective, a team today with a .377 winning percentage loses 101 games.

"It was a combination of economics and bad ownership," said Gabriel Schechter, a researcher at the National Baseball Hall of Fame and Museum.

The Phillies finished in last place 16 times in that 31-year span. They finished second-to-last seven times. They lost 100 games 12 times. In fact, they lost at least 100 games every year from 1938 to 1942. The 1941 Phillies finished 43–111 for a .279 winning percentage. They were even worse in 1942, when they finished 42–109 for a .278 winning percentage. They had one winning season in those 31 years, in 1932, when they went 78–76.

Blame ownership.

More specifically, blame Baker.

He regularly traded the team's top talent for cash. Some of the players he shipped elsewhere included Davey Bancroft, Lefty O'Doul, and Alexander. The Phillies actually sold office furniture for cash to help pay for spring training one year. In the 1920s, head groundskeeper Sam Payne had so little money to maintain the field at Baker Bowl that he got two ewes and a ram to maintain it.

Baker was so cheap that he tried to curtail Chuck Klein's power numbers. Klein's first five seasons with the Phillies might have been the best first five seasons of any player in baseball history, and that scared Baker. Baker feared Klein would move into the stratosphere of Babe Ruth, so Baker added a 20-foot screen atop the 40-foot wall in right field at Baker Bowl. The fact that Baker would take such a step to cut his best hitter's offensive production to save money—Baker thought if Klein got more money, his teammates would want more money and no doubt chaos would ensue—showed just how terribly mismanaged the Phillies were.

"I guess what stood out about Baker was his innate cheapness," Schechter said. "Extending the height of the wall in right field so Klein wouldn't hit so many home runs that he would have to pay him more, talk about cutting off your nose to spite your face. What kind of a suicidal business approach is that? That says it all. Anybody who would have the mentality to sabotage his best player, just so he wouldn't have negotiating leverage...I guess he kept files of all the bad clippings and bad press about each player. He seemed to be a one-man gang on that score.

"He seemed more interested in getting rid of players than paying them or keeping them. That started with Alexander. Baker sold him off because he was afraid Alexander was going to be drafted, which he was. So he got his money first, but selling the best pitcher in the league is not a prescription for success. Baker was pretty self-interested."

Fans responded in kind.

"Sometimes there were so few fans in the park that you'd say, 'Where is everybody? They must all be down at the shore.'" pitcher Bucky Walters said.

"Sometimes I'd go home at night after playing hard all day," shortstop Dick Bartell said. "We'd lost 10–4 or something like that, and I'd be bleeding. I'd say to myself, 'I'm just not going to do this anymore.' But I'd be back the next day, and we'd do the same thing all over again. It was really depressing."

"Win a few games in a row, and it might be cause for a congressional investigation," second baseman Danny Murtaugh said.

Baker was team president from 1913 until he died in 1930. He had deep pockets, but he wanted the team to sustain itself. Lewis Ruch ran the team from 1931 to 1932 and performed a relatively commendable job as the Phillies finished in the first division in 1932, the only time they finished there in that 31-year span. Gerry Nugent took over from 1932 to 1943, but he had an even worse run than Baker. Nugent announced he wouldn't sell off his top three players: Klein, Dick Bartell, and Pinky Whitney. But Whitney was with the Boston Braves before the end of the 1933 season, Klein was with the Chicago Cubs in 1934, and Bartell was with the New York Giants in 1935. So much for that. Nugent helped other teams so much that Harold Parrott wrote in *This Week* magazine, "Nugent makes pennants in Philadelphia, but he doesn't fly them here." But that was the only way Nugent could make ends meet: selling his top players to keep the franchise afloat.

"Those of us who weren't alive I think have a tough time appreciating how things were during the Depression in all respects," Schechter said. "I know my parents lived through it, and it just sounds horrible. How could a baseball team expect to survive if they got into a negative cycle? They didn't have players good enough to draw fans, so they didn't generate the income they needed to go get players. And how are they going to break that cycle?"

William Cox took over the franchise in 1943, but he was banned from baseball for life because he bet on Phillies games (hopefully he was smart enough to bet against them). He is one of just two owners to have been banned from baseball.

"It wasn't until the Carpenters took over and were willing to spend some money that things changed," Schechter said. "In the '30s they had one scout. That's in the whole organization. When they brought Herb Pennock in to be the GM, he brought in some people and set up a farm system. It only took them a half-dozen years to produce Richie Ashburn, Robin Roberts, Del Ennis, Willie Jones, Curt Simmons, all those guys, the whole Whiz Kids bunch. Once they got serious about being a franchise, they turned into one. They seemed strangely unwilling to do that during the '20s and '30s."

A DECADE AFTER JACKIE

Robin Roberts thinks about some of the players during his era who would have looked good in Phillies pinstripes.

Roy Campanella is one. Willie Mays is another.

"I tell ya, Henry Aaron would have looked good in our uniform, too," he said.

But the Phillies didn't sign black baseball players then. Jackie Robinson broke the color barrier with the Brooklyn Dodgers in 1947, but the Phillies waited until 1957 to integrate. And when they finally integrated, they integrated with John Kennedy, who had two hitless at-bats and played just five games before the Phillies released him. Phillies owner Robert Carpenter's unwillingness to sign black players put the organization at a competitive disadvantage for years.

Campanella signed with the Brooklyn Dodgers, Mays with the New York Giants, and Aaron with the Boston Braves, who later moved to Milwaukee. From 1947 to 1957, those three teams won the National League pennant nine times. The Phillies won the pennant in 1950, which might have been enough to convince Carpenter and general manager Herb Pennock that they didn't need black players on their roster to field a winning team.

"I think individually we thought it, but I don't remember having any discussions about it," Roberts said. "I know Campy

Jackie Robinson, left, looks over the bat Philadelphia Phillies manager Ben Chapman uses during practice as he prepares to play his first game in Philadelphia for the Dodgers on May 9, 1947. Photo courtesy of AP Images.

was from Philly. A number of guys who have played since Jackie came along have been from Philly. I'll meet them at these different events, and they'll tell me how their fathers took him to Shibe Park. And I'm thinking we could have improved our club. It did hurt the Phillies. The Red Sox were that way. The Yankees had great success, and they never signed a black player. That was the only team that didn't sign a black player that had success. The rest of us didn't. After Jackie and others started coming in, the Giants and the Dodgers and the Braves became the powerhouses. They all had key black players."

And they would lose. But that wasn't the worst of it. The Phillies treated Robinson appallingly in 1947, although no one treated him worse than manager Ben Chapman.

"Hey, you there," Chapman shouted at Robinson, according to Roger Kahn's book, *The Era*. "Snowflake. Yeah, you. You heah me. When did they let you outa jungle? Hey, we doan need no niggers here. Hey, black boy. You like white [women], black boy? You like white [women]? Which one o' the white boys' wives are you [bleep] tonight?"

Chapman's taunts disturbed Robinson's teammates. They angered Robinson, but he had to keep cool because one act of retaliation could ruin everything. But imagine looking into the Phillies' dugout and seeing players standing on the top step, pointing bats at Robinson and making machine gun sounds as he walked to the plate.

"Hate poured from the Phillies dugout," Robinson wrote in his autobiography, *I Never Had It Made*. "I felt tortured and I tried just to play ball and ignore the insults. But it was really getting to me. What did the Phillies want from me? What, indeed, did Mr. Rickey expect of me? I was, after all, a human being. What was I doing turning the cheek? For one wild and rage-crazed minute, I thought what a glorious, cleansing thing it would be to let go. To hell with the image of the patient black freak I was supposed to create. I could throw down my bat, stride over to the Phillies' dugout, grab one of those white sons of bitches and smash his teeth. The haters almost won that round."

When the Dodgers made their first trip to Philadelphia, Pennock called Dodgers general manager Branch Rickey to tell him that he could not "bring that nigger here with the rest of your team. We are just not ready for that sort of thing. We will not be able to take the field against your Brooklyn team if that boy Robinson is in uniform."

"Very well, Herbert," Rickey replied. "And if we have to claim the game by forfeit, we will do just that, I assure you."

Commissioner Happy Chandler and National League president Ford Frick warned the Phillies to stop their racial taunts.

Chapman offered to stand with Robinson for a photograph before the series, but it was a publicity stunt and nothing more.

"Mr. Rickey thought it would be gracious and generous if I posed for a picture shaking hands with Chapman," Robinson wrote. "I had to admit, though, that having my picture taken with this man was one of the most difficult things I had to make myself do. There were times, after I had bowed to humiliation like shaking hands with Chapman, when deep depression and speculation as to whether it was all worthwhile would seize me."

But Chapman and the Phillies helped unite the Dodgers. When Chapman shouted to Pee Wee Reese, "Hey Pee Wee, how ya like playin' with a...nigger?" Reese put his arm around Robinson's shoulder.

"He was a tough Southern guy," Phillies pitcher Curt Simmons said. "I remember I came up the last week of '47. I pitched the last game of the season and won a game. But the first game up, the Dodgers were in town and they had just clinched the pennant. Chapman was really on Robinson. And we had a lot of old Southern guys, too. It was a rude awakening to hear those guys get on him. The more he got on him, the more line drives he hit."

Beaten by Robinson, Chapman changed his tune the following spring.

"Let him sleep," Chapman said. "Anybody gets on him, I'm going to fine you."

Simmons chuckled as he recalled Chapman's turnaround.

"He learned his lesson about Robinson," Simmons said.

Roberts made his big-league debut with the Phillies in 1948. He said the taunting had diminished by then.

"Jackie had beaten their brains in so much that by '48 they were convinced it wasn't bothering him," Roberts said. "Although there were some individuals that still expressed that to Jackie when he came up.... Ben Chapman called Jewish people kikes. He called Italian people dagos. He called black people niggers. He had a name for all nationalities. That was Ben. If they called him a Southern so and so, he'd laugh. That was part of it. That was a way of life for him. Of course, the nigger thing didn't sit well. That really became a deal. But I know Jewish ballplayers were all kikes to Ben. And that's not just Ben. That was the way it was then."

But Roberts knew this wasn't just an in-game tactic Chapman used to rattle the opposition. He recalled how the Dodgers once swept the Phillies in a doubleheader at Ebbets Field, and that Robinson had six or seven hits in the two games. Both teams had to walk down the same runway to reach their respective clubhouses. Roberts and Simmons trailed Chapman as Robinson walked past the man who almost drove him to his breaking point.

"Robinson, you're one hell of a ballplayer," Chapman said. "But you're still a nigger."

"To live with that must have been awful for him," Roberts said of Robinson. "And Jackie just smiled and walked on by. There could have been quite a confrontation. Curt and I would have been the referees. I think we would have stood back and let it go. Jackie was a class person and a marvelous athlete."

It's just that many of the Phillies didn't treat him that way. It cost them. They wouldn't have a star black player until Richie Allen in 1964, 17 years after Robinson broke the color barrier.

BAKER BOWL

There is a scene in the movie *Groundhog Day* when Bill Murray's character Phil Connors says, "I have been stabbed, shot, poisoned, frozen, hung, electrocuted, and burned."

There could have been a similar line for Baker Bowl.

It was mocked, burned, damned, condemned, rotted, ridiculed, and deadly. It didn't start out that way. Baker Bowl, built for $101,000 in 1887 and originally known as Philadelphia Base Ball Grounds or Huntingdon Street Grounds, sat inside the borders of Broad Street, Lehigh Avenue, 15th Street, and Huntingdon Avenue in North Philadelphia. In its infancy, it had been praised for being a masterpiece because it used brick instead of wood, which had been used exclusively to build other ballparks.

But the brick structure wasn't its only distinguishing characteristic. It also had unusual dimensions. The original dimensions

The Baker Bowl was a hitter's dream and a pitcher's nightmare.

had the left-field fence more than 400 feet away from home plate, center field 408 feet away, and right field just 300 feet away. Eventually, left field stood a more manageable 341½ feet from home plate, although right field moved in to 272 feet and eventually out to 280½ feet. To try to make the ballpark a little more fair in right field—which proved to be a hopeless cause—Baker Bowl had a 40-foot tin wall that ultimately became a 60-foot wall topped with a 20-foot screen. To put that into perspective, the Green Monster at Fenway Park stands just 37 feet tall and sits 310 feet from home plate down the line.

Phillies owner William Baker, who renamed the ballpark after himself shortly after he purchased the club in 1913, added a screen atop the wall in 1929 because he said, "Home runs have become too cheap at the Philadelphia ballpark." Of course, others correctly suspected that Baker added the screen because it would cut Chuck Klein's home-run total, which would allow Baker to pay him less.

Hitters, particularly left-handed hitters, loved playing at Baker Bowl because almost anything hit in the air would float over the wall for a cheap home run. Other balls simply would hit off the wall for a single or double. The wall made Klein a Hall of Famer.

"It might be exaggerating to say the outfield wall casts a shadow across the infield," legendary sportswriter Red Smith wrote. "But if the right fielder had eaten onions at lunch, the second baseman knew it."

So while hitters loved the wall, pitchers loathed it. And right fielders found their job a whole lot easier.

"Playing right field in Baker Bowl was the softest job in baseball," said Casey Stengel, who played for the Phillies from 1920 to 1921. "I had the wall behind me and the second baseman in front of me. The foul line was on my left, Cy Williams, the center fielder, was on my right. The only time I had a chance to catch the ball was when it was hit right at me."

The ballpark had other memorable traits in addition to the wall. It had a Lifebuoy soap advertisement that stretched across the wall from 1928 to 1938. "The Phillies use Lifebuoy," the sign read. It didn't take long for a prankster to scrawl on the bottom, "And they still stink." Baker Bowl kept its clubhouses in center field, one of just three ballparks to have that feature. The Phillies eventually moved from the first-floor clubhouse to the second-floor clubhouse, with visiting teams taking up the bare accommodations on the first floor. The second-floor clubhouse had a pool that eventually had to be drained because it began to fall apart. Players hung their clothes on nails. The dugouts had no bathrooms, which meant players had to run to the clubhouse in center field if they had to go.

As bad as the accommodations were, the Phillies had their moments at Baker Bowl. They played their first World Series there in 1915. Pitcher Grover Cleveland Alexander and the Phillies beat the Boston Red Sox 3–1 in Game 1, although the Phillies would not win again as the Red Sox won the best-of-seven Series in just five games. President Woodrow Wilson attended Game 2 of the 1915 World Series, which made him the first president to attend a World Series game—and the only president to ever set foot in Baker Bowl. Red Donahue no-hit the Boston Braves 5–0 on July 8, 1898, the only no-hitter the Phillies threw at Baker Bowl. Babe Ruth played his final game for the Boston Braves there on May 30, 1935.

But then there were the disasters.

Fire completely destroyed the park on August 6, 1894. Remarkably, nobody was injured. Phillies owner Al Reach, who feared another fire, built the new ballpark mostly of steel and brick, which made it a modern marvel. But those good feelings lasted for only 10 years. On August 8, 1903, mayhem struck. Just outside the ballpark on 15th Street during the second game of a doubleheader, a couple drunks got into an altercation with some young girls. One of the drunks grabbed one of the girls and tumbled on top of her. The girls cried for help, which caught the attention of fans along the left-field line. Fans poured onto a balcony that extended 30 feet high over 15th Street to see what was going on. But the wooden deck, which had been supported by rotted timbers underneath, couldn't handle the weight and collapsed.

"In the twinkling of an eye, the street was piled four deep with bleeding, injured, shrieking humanity struggling amid the piling debris," the *Philadelphia Inquirer* reported.

Twelve people died, and 232 people were injured.

But that wasn't the only time the ballpark collapsed. It happened again May 14, 1927. Fans had scurried underneath the roof of the lower deck on the first-base side to stay dry from rain, but the section couldn't support the additional people and collapsed. Fifty people were injured, and one man died from a heart attack. A girder had rotted and couldn't hold the additional people.

After the fire in 1894, the Phillies played at the University of Pennsylvania's University Field until they could return. After the first collapse in 1903, the Phillies played at the Philadelphia Athletics' Columbia Park. And after the second collapse in 1927, the Phillies played at Shibe Park.

Baker Bowl had neared its end. The Phillies played their last game there in 1938.

"It was beautifully decrepit," newspaper reporter Edgar Williams said. "They don't make ballparks like that anymore."

IN THE CLUTCH

BREAK ON THROUGH

Mike Schmidt already had established himself as a star before Pete Rose joined the Phillies in 1979.

He had hit 171 home runs from 1974 to 1978, the most in baseball. He had 497 RBIs, fourth-most in baseball behind Steve Garvey (514), George Foster (509), and Rusty Staub (501). He had finished in the top 10 in National League Most Valuable Player voting in 1974, 1976, and 1977.

He was a stud. It's just that Schmidt didn't always feel that way.

Enter Rose.

"My biggest project, although I didn't look at it as a project, was Mike Schmidt," Rose said. "Because when I went to Philadelphia for the '79 season, I believed that Mike Schmidt was the greatest player in the league. And I wanted to make him understand that, other than hitting home runs every day, there are other ways to lead a team. What he did is, he became a leader defensively. He became a leader with his base-running. He became a leader with his knowledge of the game. And everyone just followed suit."

It came together in the biggest and most important year of his Hall of Fame career in 1980. The Phillies had fallen short in the NL Championship Series in 1976, 1977, and 1978. They missed the playoffs completely in 1979. A core of homegrown talent that

Mike Schmidt bats during a game against the Pittsburgh Pirates in July 1980 in Philadelphia.

included Schmidt, Greg Luzinski, Larry Bowa, and Bob Boone understood they had one more shot to prove they could win a World Series.

If they failed in '80?

Poof.

Gone.

Schmidt started to believe Rose when he told him that he was the best player in the game. He responded with a career year, hitting .286 with 48 home runs and 121 RBIs to win MVP honors.

Rose played a major part in that. He took pressure off Schmidt, who felt free to experiment with his stance in '79.

"I wanted a stance that gave me a strike zone like Pete Rose's and that produced balls hit with power to all fields, much like the late Roberto Clemente," Schmidt said. "Clemente stood off the plate because he liked the ball out and away, on the outside corner. Having to force his upper body to go out after the ball was what felt right to him. That same is true for Rose, and I thought it would suit me best as a hitter, too. So I backed up about eight inches off the plate and moved a bit deeper in the box. From that position, I could stride into the plate instead of striding toward the pitcher. That forced me to take my left shoulder into the ball, rather than to open up, allowing me to hit the ball more to center and to the right- and left-center-field gaps than down the left side."

Schmidt then resigned as team captain before the '80 season so Rose could have the job.

"You've got Pete Rose, who exemplifies what a captain ought to be," Schmidt said. "Me, I'm a lot less outgoing."

Phillies manager Dallas Green instead left the job vacant. But it seemed clear that Schmidt enjoyed Rose's presence in the clubhouse and the mental boost he provided.

"If he didn't hit a home run, he'd get down on himself," Rose said. "It's not what you did in the last at-bat, it's what you do in the next at-bat. And that next year he won the MVP for the season and the World Series. He did exactly what he was supposed to do."

The Phillies entered the final series of the '80 season in a first-place tie with the Montreal Expos in the NL East. Schmidt went

THE MVPS

The Baseball Writers' Association of America has named five Phillies the National League Most Valuable Player:

- Chuck Klein in 1932.
- Jim Konstanty in 1950.
- Mike Schmidt in 1980, 1981, and 1986.
- Ryan Howard in 2006.
- Jimmy Rollins in 2007.

2-for-2 with a sacrifice fly and a solo home run to lead the Phillies to a 2–1 victory in the October 3 series opener against the Expos at Olympic Stadium to give the Phillies a one-game lead with two games to play. He came up even bigger the next afternoon. He went 3-for-5 with a two-run home run in the top of the eleventh inning in a 6–4 victory to clinch the division.

Schmidt hit just .208 in the NLCS against the Houston Astros, which didn't silence critics that he came up small in big situations. But he hit .381 with two homers and seven RBIs in the World Series against the Kansas City Royals to win World Series MVP honors.

He had silenced his critics for good.

"The last few weeks of the regular season, as well as the World Series, were special for me because I put to rest any question about my ability to deliver when our team needed the big hit," Schmidt said. "1980 was the year I was finally recognized as a clutch player."

It also was the year he was noted as a winner.

"Sometimes you'll hear one player saying about another, 'He's good, but he's never been on a winner,'" Schmidt said. "No matter how many home-run titles you win, it means little if you're not part of a winning team. In Philadelphia and in my case individually, I didn't get that label until the 1980 World Series."

Schmidt learned after the season about his NL MVP award. He made sure to thank Rose.

"Pete instilled in me a new vitality for playing the game at this point in my career," he said. "Being 31 years old, which is a turning point for a lot of ballplayers, he gave me a great outlook on the game of baseball, a feeling of youth, and a feeling of wanting to have fun on the baseball field. Pete came along at a great time in my career, and I'm thankful for that."

Probably just as thankful as those championship-starved Phillies fans.

WAIT UNTIL '08? THINK AGAIN

Pat Gillick stood behind a podium at Citizens Bank Park on July 30, 2006, and told reporters that he didn't think it would be practical to expect the Phillies to contend until 2008.

"Realistically, I think it would be a stretch to think we're going to be there in '07," he said. "I don't want to mislead anyone. I think it's going to be a little slower."

The Phillies pulled the plug on their season that afternoon when they traded Bobby Abreu and Cory Lidle to the New York Yankees in a salary dump. In days prior, they had shipped catcher Sal Fasano to the Yankees and David Bell to the Milwaukee Brewers. In days following, they shipped Rheal Cormier to the Cincinnati Reds and Ryan Franklin to the St. Louis Cardinals. But with those comments, Gillick told fans to forget about 2007.

Now where's that season-ticket renewal form?

Phillies 2007: Wait until 2008. No, really, wait until 2008.

The '06 breakup made sense to Gillick. The Phillies had spent millions in recent seasons to pick up Jim Thome, Billy Wagner, Kevin Millwood, Eric Milton, Tim Worrell, and Bell. It got them nowhere, other than some entertaining but ultimately failed pursuits of the National League wild card in 2003 and 2005.

"We haven't won with this group," Gillick said. "So consequently, I think you've got to change the mix."

Gillick wanted to start with a clean slate. The Phillies were 49–54 on July 30, 13½ games behind the New York Mets in the NL East and five games behind the Reds in the wild-card race. Moving some veterans would allow younger players like Jimmy Rollins, Chase Utley, and Ryan Howard to assert themselves in the clubhouse. It also would give players like Shane Victorino an opportunity to play.

It was supposed to take time for all that to develop, but Howard couldn't wait for '08. He wanted to win in '06.

He was hitting .287 with 35 home runs and 87 RBIs on July 30. His 35 homers led the National League. His 87 RBIs ranked fourth. But then he blew up in August. He had 14 homers with 41 RBIs to earn National League Player of the Month honors. His 41 RBIs were the most by a player in any month in any league since Frank Howard had 41 RBIs for the Los Angeles Dodgers in July 1962. Howard, who had won NL Rookie of the Year honors in 2005, hit .358 with 23 homers and 62 RBIs from July 31 through the end of the season as the Phillies vaulted into NL wild-card contention.

So well had the Phillies recovered from their fire sale that 12 days after they sent Franklin to the Cardinals, Gillick changed course and acquired Jamie Moyer from the Seattle Mariners on August 19.

"We've said that we were buyers and sellers," Gillick insisted. "At that point, we were sellers. The way we've played since the July 31 deadline puts us in a different position."

Three days later they picked up Jose Hernandez from the Pittsburgh Pirates. Five days after that they picked up Jeff Conine from the Baltimore Orioles. Howard kept the Phillies within striking range of the wild card until reinforcements arrived. His 23 homers after the Abreu trade were four more than any other player in baseball. His 62 RBIs were seven more than any other player in baseball. And only Miguel Cabrera (.369), Carlos Guillen (.365), and Robinson Cano (.365) hit better than Howard in that stretch.

Howard became one of the most feared hitters in baseball. Cincinnati Reds manager Jerry Narron intentionally walked Howard three times on August 11 at Citizens Bank Park. It wasn't a complete surprise. Because of a double-switch earlier, the Phillies had the pitcher hitting behind him. But it still

In the game against the Washington Nationals on August 31, 2006, at RFK Stadium in Washington D.C., Ryan Howard waits for a pitch before hitting his 49th home run of the season that gave him the Phillies single-season record, previously held by Hall of Famer Mike Schmidt.

raised a few eyebrows when Narron intentionally walked Howard to load the bases with no outs, putting the winning run at third base, in the bottom of the fourteenth inning.

"He's in scoring position when he steps in the box," Narron explained.

Two batters later, Aaron Rowand singled home the winning run in a 6–5 victory.

Houston Astros manager Phil Garner intentionally walked Howard to lead off the ninth inning in a 3–2 loss in 10 innings to the Phillies on September 4.

"It was gutsy," Utley said.

"I wasn't surprised," Charlie Manuel said.

The Phillies had a half-game lead over the Los Angeles Dodgers in the wild-card race with just seven games to play. But the Phillies stumbled and finished 3–4 while the Dodgers went

ROOKIES OF THE YEAR

The Baseball Writers' Association of America has named four Phillies the National League Rookie of the Year:

- Jack Sanford in 1957.
- Richie Allen in 1964.
- Scott Rolen in 1997.
- Ryan Howard in 2005.

6–0 to clinch it. The Phillies missed the playoffs, but Howard had cemented his status as one of the most fearsome hitters in the game. He hit .313 with 58 homers and 149 RBIs. He got 20 first-place votes to beat St. Louis Cardinals first baseman Albert Pujols 388–347 for NL Most Valuable Player.

"I never would have thought it would happen this fast," he said.

"He's better than I expected," Gillick said. "Our people thought he would struggle against left-handed pitching. That's why we tried to sign Wes Helms and Eddie Perez last year. We were looking for someone to take the heat off him with a left-hander pitching. As it turned out, none of that was necessary."

It wasn't necessary to wait until 2008, either. Howard proved he was more than capable of helping the Phillies win now.

WE'RE THE TEAM TO BEAT

Every January the Phillies fly a handful of players from their off-season homes to Philadelphia for their annual winter caravan.

The caravan is free publicity for the Phillies during their slowest month of the year. The Phillies already have made their major roster moves for the upcoming season, and they're still a few weeks away from spring training in Clearwater, Florida. January typically is quiet, except for the occasional waiver-wire signing or minor trade. And that is why the Phillies ask players to show up, talk to the media, and meet some fans before they fly to Florida in a few weeks.

Typically, nothing happens at these events. It's cheesesteaks and clichés.

"We're excited for the season."

"We like our pitching staff."

"We like our lineup."

"We feel we have a championship-caliber ballclub."

Blah, blah, blah.

But that changed in 2007, when Jimmy Rollins made a bold proclamation.

"For the first time since I've been here, I think we are the team to beat in the National League East," he said. "I know we are. Finally."

Say what? The Phillies finished second in the NL East in 2006—12 games behind the New York Mets. Most people would think New York would be the team to beat for that very reason. Or the Braves, who had won 14 consecutive division titles before the Mets snapped their streak. The Phillies? They hadn't won anything since 1993 and had fallen just short of the postseason in three of the previous four years. But that didn't stop Rollins from making his declaration. And it didn't take long for his words to reach New York.

"I was surprised how it just kind of started withering all over the place," said Gigi Rollins, Jimmy's mother. "But the bottom line is you make a statement, you need to back it up. You better make sure you can back it up. I've always told him, 'Listen, if you can talk the talk, you better be able to back up whatever you say.'"

Rollins didn't say those words to disrespect the Mets or Braves. He said those words because he liked his team. The Phillies made one of the biggest moves of the off-season, acquiring Freddy Garcia from the Chicago White Sox to bolster the rotation. They added a few other pieces he also thought would help. Rollins simply wanted to express confidence in his teammates. He wanted everybody to believe. The New York media painted a different picture.

Jimmy Rollins bats during a game against the San Francisco Giants at Citizens Bank Park on June 4, 2006, in Philadelphia.

J-Roll is saying the Mets stink!
How dare he?

It put a bull's-eye on Rollins' back that lasted until the final game of the regular season.

"The New York media really ran with that," said James Rollins, Jimmy's father. "So he was always in the spotlight. The whole year. The team to beat. The team to beat. The team to beat. He just wanted to push his teammates. I was like, 'I hope this works out.' And it did work out."

Rollins earned National League Most Valuable Player honors after he became the first player in baseball history to have 200 hits, 20 doubles, 20 triples, 20 home runs, and 20 stolen bases in a season. He is one of just four players to have 20 doubles, 20 triples, 20 home runs, and 20 stolen bases with Frank Schulte (1911 Chicago Cubs), Willie Mays (1957 New York Giants), and Curtis Granderson (2007 Detroit Tigers). He won his first Gold Glove and Silver Slugger awards. And he did it with a lot of pressure on him. Every time the Phillies slipped, the media found Rollins in the clubhouse and asked him about it. *What do you think of your chances now? Change your mind yet on that whole "team to beat" thing? Wish you hadn't said it?*

That proved especially true when the Phillies opened the season 4–11 for the worst record in baseball. But Rollins never shied away. He answered the questions. He never backed off.

"Jimmy kind of feeds off pressure," Gigi said. "It doesn't bother him to be in a pressure situation, because all his life he grew up in those situations. So for him that was normal. He feeds off that. It didn't bother him. He made the statement, he knew he had to back it up, but he didn't put pressure on himself to back it up. He knew what he had to go out there and do."

"You respect the competition," James said. "But you never show them you're scared."

Rollins hit .296 with 38 doubles, 20 triples, 30 home runs, 94 RBIs, and 41 stolen bases, hitting primarily out of the leadoff spot for the Phillies. He set career-highs in games (162); runs (139); hits (212); triples, home runs, RBIs, and extra-base hits (88); and at-bats (716). He led the league in at-bats, runs, and triples. He set NL records for runs and extra-base hits for a shortstop. He set major-league records for plate appearances (778) and at-bats (716). His 212 hits were the most for a Phillie since Dave Cash had 213 in 1975.

But most important, he carried a team after he became Public Enemy No. 1 in New York.

"I'm not afraid," Rollins said. "Either you're going to mess up, or you're going to be great, right? And if you don't mess up, you'll never be great. At least if you never try to mess up, you'll never know if you can be great. I remember my basketball coach in high school, he always said, 'You never want to go through your life saying *if*: If I would have tried harder. If I wouldn't have been afraid. If this. If that.' And when he said it, I was like, that's pretty good. If you do something, find out what you can and can't do."

Rollins could make a prediction, put a bull's-eye on his back, and deliver the goods. That certainly weighed on the minds of MVP voters. Rollins received 16 first-place votes, Colorado Rockies left fielder Matt Holliday received 11, and Milwaukee Brewers first baseman Prince Fielder received five. Rollins edged Holliday 353 to 336.

"I'm sure that was motivation for sure," Rollins said. "It kept me focused. When you are focused, you are motivated. When you're not motivated, you start losing focus. They run hand in hand. They're basically the same thing."

Rollins had a little extra motivation during the final game of the 2007 season. The Phillies needed to beat the Washington Nationals to clinch at least a tie for the NL East title and force a one-game playoff with the Mets. Rollins also needed one more triple for 20, which would turn a remarkable season into a historic one. He got the triple in the sixth inning of that 6–1 victory over the Nationals that sent the Phillies to the postseason for the first time since 1993. Of all the memorable moments Rollins had in 2007, his 20th triple sticks out most.

"When he hit it in the corner, I was like, 'He's got to be going,'" James said. "I knew he wasn't going to stop. It was the perfect scenario. He ran hard and hustled for it. What more can you ask for? It was a stamp. It was a stamp on the season. We loved it. You couldn't ask for anything better than that."

It stamped a season that made Rollins the greatest shortstop in Phillies history.

"I know he's always wanted to make a difference," Gigi said. "You hear a lot of people say, 'I never would have thought my son would have made it to the MLB.' I had no doubt Jimmy would make it, because that's something he wanted his entire life, and he worked hard for that. I knew if given the opportunity, he was going to make it. But for him to be MVP? Now I can say I truly never thought he would do that. That was just something that we never discussed."

They can talk about it today. And maybe in the future they can talk about the Hall of Fame. Rollins enters the 2010 season with 1,629 hits in his first nine-plus seasons. If he stays healthy and productive, he could make a run at 3,000 hits.

"He's carving his way there," Gigi said. "When you really look back and see what he's done over the years, he's doing something that is making a difference."

And that's all Jimmy wanted in the first place.

KING COLE

Everything changed for Cole Hamels in October 2008.

He already had been one of the more successful pitchers in Phillies history before the '08 postseason. He was 38–23 with a 3.43 ERA in nearly three seasons in the majors. His .623 winning percentage ranked third in franchise history for pitchers with at least 60 decisions. Only Grover Cleveland Alexander, who went 190–91 (.676) from 1911 to 1917 and in 1930, and Tom Seaton, who went 43-24 (.642) from 1912 to 1913, had better marks. But Hamels elevated his stature the way pitchers like Curt Schilling, Bob Gibson, John Smoltz, and Josh Beckett had elevated theirs. He went 4–0 with a 1.80 ERA in the '08 playoffs. He became one of just 12 pitchers in baseball history to win four games in a single postseason. He had a chance to become the first pitcher to have five wins—with every appearance coming as a starter—but fell short in Game 5 of the World Series when Ryan Madson allowed a game-tying solo home run to Rocco Baldelli in the seventh inning of an eventual 4–3 victory.

Hamels still won World Series MVP honors after he won the National League Championship Series MVP award. Had he earned the Big-Game Pitcher label?

"Shoot, I guess so," Hamels said. "I love to go out there and pitch. I love to go out there and win. That's all I strive for."

Here is what made Hamels' postseason so special. He pitched Game 1 of the National League Division Series against the Milwaukee Brewers, Game 1 of the NLCS against the Los Angeles Dodgers, and Game 1 of the World Series against the Tampa Bay Rays. He got the win each time, giving the Phillies the lead in every series. He picked up the win in Game 5 of the NLCS, when the Phillies clinched their first National League pennant since 1993. He pitched well in comically bad conditions in the first half of Game 5 of the World Series, which was postponed 46 hours in the middle of the sixth inning because of rain.

"I think they believe in me when I take the mound, but I believe in them behind me," Hamels said. "We believe in each other."

Hamels took the loss against the Colorado Rockies in Game 1 of the 2007 NLDS, when the Rockies swept the Phillies in the best-of-five series. Hamels seemed determined to get the Phillies started in the right direction in 2008. And he did when he threw eight shutout innings against the Brewers.

"I had the understanding of what it is when you do win the first game, the momentum that it causes, especially at home," he said. "When we scored those runs, I think they did have the confidence I wasn't going to allow any more runs."

In Game 1 of the NLCS, Hamels allowed two runs in seven innings to pick up the win in a 3–2 victory. The Dodgers actually scored a run in the first and a run in the fourth to take a 2–0 lead, but Hamels toughened up and held the Dodgers scoreless in his final three innings while the Phillies scored three runs in the sixth to take the lead. Hamels was asked after the game if he thought he was building a reputation as a big-game pitcher.

CY YOUNGS

The Baseball Writers' Association of America has named three Phillies the National League Cy Young Award winner:

- Steve Carlton in 1972, 1977, 1980, and 1982.
- John Denny in 1983.
- Steve Bedrosian in 1987.

"I hope so," he said. "I'm going to go out there, any and every opportunity that Charlie [Manuel] gives me with the ball, I'm going to go out there, try to win, and pitch deep in the game to allow the team to win. I think that's all Charlie can ask of me and that's all I can ask of myself is go out there, play as hard as I possibly can, and hopefully at the end of the day we have a *W*."

Hamels allowed one run in seven innings in Game 5 of the NLCS to clinch the NL pennant and series MVP honors, going 2–0 with a 1.93 ERA. Hamels had guided the Phillies through the NLDS and NLCS, but the World Series would be the ultimate challenge. Almost every baseball expert had picked the Rays to beat the Phillies in the World Series. But those experts underestimated how dominating Hamels could be.

"I think his poise and his focus and his determination plays a big part in who he is and how he pitches," Manuel said. "Cole Hamels goes out there and you can tell, he can smell a win and he's going to get you there. And he'll give you everything he's got. And basically that's what I like about him. I mean, you can walk out there and he knows—I think he knows just about how far he's going to go. But most of all, I like his focus and his determination and his coolness. Cole is cocky in a good way. And that's a positive, strong way."

The Phillies had a 3–1 lead in the best-of-seven series when Hamels started Game 5 of the World Series on October 27. He opened with three scoreless innings when the rain started to fall with the Phillies holding a 2–0 lead. He allowed a run in the fourth to make it 2–1. In ridiculous conditions in the sixth, Hamels allowed another run to tie the game.

Hamels deserved better. He deserved the win. He didn't get it, but the fact that he pitched well in terrible conditions in Game 5 might have swayed voters to name him World Series MVP.

"I can't describe it," Hamels said. "It's such a phenomenal experience."

A MIDSUMMER NIGHT'S DREAM

Before 1964 became *nineteen-freaking-sixty-four*, Johnny Callison hit a home run at the All-Star Game at Shea Stadium that convinced Phillies fans it was going to be their year.

The American League held a 4–3 lead over the National League in the bottom of the ninth inning on July 7, when Willie Mays worked a leadoff walk against Boston Red Sox reliever Dick Radatz. Mays stole second and scored the tying run on Orlando Cepeda's bloop single, with Cepeda advancing to second on an error. Ken Boyer popped out to third for the first out. Radatz intentionally walked Johnny Edwards to put runners on first and second to set up the double play. He struck out Hank Aaron for the second out.

Callison, borrowing a bat from Billy Williams, stepped into the batter's box with a chance to win it. He was 0-for-2 since entering the game as a pinch-hitter for Jim Bunning in the fifth inning.

"A lot of guys didn't want to hit against Radatz," Callison said. "To tell the truth, I wasn't too crazy about it, either."

But the hard-throwing Radatz threw Callison a first-pitch fastball, and Callison jumped on it.

"I swung at the first pitch," Callison said. "I wasn't about to let him work on me. Fortunately, I happened to hit it solid. Oh, yeah, I knew it was gone. You can tell."

It was a three-run homer that won the All-Star Game in an era when it really, truly mattered to the players. Callison won All-Star

MVP honors and probably would have won National League MVP honors had the Phillies not blown the pennant with 12 games to play.

"It's probably the biggest thrill I had in baseball," Callison said. "In the All-Star Game, you're out there with the best there is. Just being there is an honor. But to hit the winning home run in the ninth inning...I mean, what more could a player want? As a kid, you dream about someday playing in the World Series and you dream about playing in the All-Star Game. I got one. I didn't get the other."

It was interesting how Callison got to that moment. He made the team as a reserve and understandably so with a starting out-field that included Mays, Williams, and Roberto Clemente. Callison thought he would get only one at-bat—his pinch-hit at-bat for Bunning in the fifth.

"I thought I was done," he said. "I was surprised when [manager Walter] Alston let me in to play right field."

Especially because Alston had Aaron on the bench. But Aaron was sick.

"That's the only reason I got in," Callison said.

The AL took a one-run lead in the seventh inning when future Phillies manager Jim Fregosi's sacrifice fly scored Frank Howard. Radatz entered in the bottom of the seventh. Radatz was an imposing figure on the mound at 6'6" and 250 pounds. He wasn't easy to hit with a 97-mph fastball that he threw side-armed. Callison flied out to Mickey Mantle in deep right-center field in the seventh.

"I tagged one pretty good then, too," Callison said. "When I hit it, I thought it had a chance."

Fast-forward to the ninth inning. Mays caught a break on a 2–2 slider that home-plate umpire Ed Sudol called a ball.

"I had him struck out," Radatz said. "Willie knew it, too. He was walking back to the dugout."

Radatz lost his composure for a second as Cepeda hit the bloop single to right. It set up Callison, who followed Aaron. Aaron struck out on three straight fastballs.

"He really hummed them past Hank," Callison said. "I also remembered how hard he threw in the seventh. So, I decided to switch to a lighter bat."

He switched to Williams' lumber. We know what happened next.

"Stayed fair by 10 feet," he said. "I floated around the bases."

NUMBERS DON'T LIE
[OR DO THEY?]

NUMBER 500!

Don Robinson faced Mike Schmidt 74 times in his 15-year career.

The only hitter he faced more than Schmidt was Hall of Fame shortstop Ozzie Smith, whom he faced 84 times.

Robinson knew Schmidt well, and he dominated him throughout his career. He allowed just nine hits in 60 at-bats against Schmidt for a .150 average. He walked him 13 times. He struck him out 14 times. But on the rare occurrences when Schmidt connected, he made it count. He had seven extra-base hits against Robinson, five of which were home runs. And of those five home runs, the last home run he smacked off Robinson was the biggest.

It was Schmidt's 500th career home run, which he hit April 18, 1987, at Three Rivers Stadium in Pittsburgh.

"My 500th homer was a fun period," Schmidt said. "I had just come off of my third MVP year, so my confidence was high and my hitting approach was one that prevented me from an extended slump due to focusing on home runs."

The Phillies had blown a 5–2 lead in the bottom of the eighth inning to hand the Pirates a one-run lead entering the ninth. Milt Thompson hit a one-out single, but was out at second on a force out. Juan Samuel stole second and moved to third on a wild pitch. Robinson walked Von Hayes to put runners at the corners with two outs.

Pirates manager Jim Leyland visited the mound with Schmidt coming up. Intentional walk?

"No," Leyland said. "I got my veteran, Robinson, out there. I know he's not going to give in to him."

But be careful with Schmidt? Absolutely.

"He's going to hit a home run," Hayes told Pirates first baseman Sid Bream. "It's perfect. Everything's in order."

"No way," Bream replied.

Robinson ran the count to 3–0. Hayes took a short lead.

"You think he'll be swinging?" Bream asked Hayes.

"You better believe it," Hayes said. "He's going to hit his 500th right here."

"No, he isn't."

"Yes, he is."

Schmidt crushed Robinson's 3–0 fastball over the left-field wall for a three-run home run for not only the 500th of his career, but a two-out, game-winning home run in the ninth inning. It couldn't have been better unless it had happened on the final day of the season at Veterans Stadium and had clinched the Phillies the division.

"As soon as he hit it, there was no doubt," Robinson said.

"I just think for special athletes there are special dramatics," Leyland said.

Schmidt became just the 14th player in baseball history to hit 500 home runs. At the time, hitting 500 homers was a more difficult milestone to reach than getting 3,000 hits, which had been accomplished 16 times, or 300 wins, which had been accomplished 19 times.

How times have changed. Eleven players have since reached 500 home runs for a total of 25 players. Eleven players have since reached 3,000 hits for a total of 27, and five players have since reached 300 wins for a total of 24. Back then, some thought Schmidt might be the last player to hit 500 homers in the 20th century. Schmidt actually thought he might be the last hitter ever to hit 500, period.

"I could possibly be the last guy to ever do it," he said that day. "And one reason is that the science of pitching today—compared

THE GENTLEMAN

Willie Mays faced countless pitchers in his Hall of Fame career, but there are few people in baseball he respected more than Robin Roberts.

Mays made his big-league debut against the Phillies on May 25, 1951. He went 0-for-5 that day and 0-for-12 in the series. It was a poor start, but Mays remembered that Roberts made sure he felt comfortable. Five years after Jackie Robinson broke baseball's color barrier in 1947, things were still difficult for black players.

"I thought it was just a wonderful feeling when a guy from another team could come up to me like Roberts did," Mays said. "And he had been there quite a while before I got there. Roberts was always out there by himself, and he would always make sure everything was right. If something was wrong, he would come over. One day we were playing in Philadelphia and I stole second. Roberts thought I was calling the pitches to [Willie] McCovey from second base, but I wasn't. But I pretended I was. So Robbie got mad and he came halfway over to me and said, 'What are you doing calling the pitches?' I said, 'Robbie, I'm not calling the pitches. And if you think that, tell the catcher to change signs.' The next day he called me and said, 'I apologize. I shouldn't do that.' Yeah, he called me. That's why I say he's such a classy guy. Whatever you did he was always there and he remembered all the things that he did wrong. He was a nice man."

with the styles of hitting—is not conducive to long careers or high home-run totals. I think these guys like [Oakland's Jose] Canseco and [Texas' Pete] Incaviglia—guys who are hell-bent on hitting home runs every time they walk up there—are going to have to adjust. Because pitching nowadays will eat up guys like that. The science of pitching and relief pitching being what it is, I think those guys are going to have a hard time staying consistent hitting home runs. What made me a consistent home-run hitter over my career was that I constantly fought to develop a batting stroke that wasn't like that—like that big, long, big-stride uppercut.

"Those guys hit 30 home runs with that style. But they also strike out 180 times, and they hit 140 or 150 balls in the air to the warning track that are caught. I say [change] that uppercut swing and turn 75 of those long fly balls into gappers or into singles or into valuable hits for their team and keep their home-run production the same. And they'll find they have more fun playing the game, and they're apt to stay around for a longer time."

10,000 LOSSES

The easiest pick? Pick the Phillies last every time.

That is how Phillies chairman Bill Giles filled out his National League standings every year as a child in Cincinnati. Giles grew up in the Queen City, where his father, Warren Giles, served as president and general manager of the Reds from 1937 to 1951. He recalled how every spring a Cincinnati newspaper asked Reds fans to predict the final standings in the National League. Predict every team's finish in correct order and win a prize. There were just eight teams then: the Boston Braves, Brooklyn Dodgers, Chicago Cubs, Cincinnati Reds, New York Giants, Pittsburgh Pirates, St. Louis Cardinals, and the Phillies.

Picking the eight teams wasn't easy, except one.

"I always started out picking the Phillies last," Giles chuckled.

He didn't exactly crawl out on a limb. The Phillies finished in last place 16 times from 1918 to 1949. They finished in seventh place eight times and sixth place four times. So in a span of 31 years, the Phillies finished sixth or lower in the National League an astonishing 28 times. They lost 100 or more games 12 times in that 31-year span. That is some pretty horrific baseball. It is a borderline miracle the Phillies remained in business all those years. They averaged just 343,810 fans a year in that span, an average of just 4,465 fans a game. Minor-league teams today do better business than that. Of course, they also put a better product on the field.

No wonder the Phillies became the first team in professional sports history to lose 10,000 games. They accomplished that milestone July 15, 2007, in a 10–2 loss to the St. Louis Cardinals at Citizens Bank Park.

"I don't know much about 10,000 losses," manager Charlie Manuel said. "I try to concentrate on the wins."

Phillies fans hold up the total number of losses the team will have notched in franchise history—10,000—on the day the team lost to the Colorado Rockies in a game on July 8, 2007, in Denver. Philadelphia's 10,000 losses were the most by any team in any sport. Photo courtesy of AP Images.

The buildup to that milestone was one of the more bizarre moments in Phillies history. Fans actually celebrated their team's futility. They dedicated websites to it, counting down losses like Dick Clark counts down seconds at Times Square on New Year's Eve. Fans made commemorative T-shirts. They cheered as Ryan Howard struck out to end the game.

"I'm definitely glad it's over," Howard said. "I just thought there was too much press about it."

There was. Current Phillies like Howard, Chase Utley, and Jimmy Rollins were bemused at the questions leading up to the 10,000[th] loss. They had nothing to do with it. In fact, players like Utley and Howard never have been on a losing team.

WHAT? ME WORRY?

Pete Rose put baseball first and everything else second.

He put that mantra to the test in 1979, his first season with the Phillies. Rose was hitting .312 with 36 doubles, four triples, four home runs, and 56 RBIs after a 15–2 loss to the Chicago Cubs at Wrigley Field on September 9. Two days later, before the Phillies opened a three-game series against the New York Mets at Shea Stadium, Rose's wife, Karolyn, filed for divorce.

People like to think baseball players shove their personal distractions aside better than others, but divorce, death, breakups, whatever, affect them too. Relief pitcher Tim Worrell left the Phillies for personal reasons in May 2005. His problems affected him. He was 0–1 with a 9.82 ERA in his first 14 appearances before he left the team for almost two months. He returned in July but asked to be released or traded so he could be closer to his family in Arizona. He got his wish.

Rose never let his off-the-field problems affect him. He got served divorce papers and went 3-for-4 with a walk, RBI, and a run scored that night against the Mets. But that's not the most impressive part. Rose, who could have been forgiven for being distracted the final month of the '79 season, hit .676 (23-for-34) with three doubles, one triple, two RBIs, and 10 walks in the nine games after he got served.

"How the hell do you do it?" Greg Luzinski asked Rose. "You just got served divorce papers? You're going through a divorce. I don't understand it."

Rose thought about it.

"Let me tell you something, Greg," Rose said. "If you know you're going to get divorced, are you better off hitting .330 or .230?"

"I guess that makes sense," Luzinski said.

From the time Karolyn filed for divorce to the end of the season, Rose hit .458 to raise his average from .312 to .331 to finish second in the National League in hitting behind Keith Hernandez, who hit .344.

"Why am I going to let what's happening to me off the field affect my teammates, the fans I play in front of, my organization, and me as a baseball player?" Rose said. "I can't let that affect me because everybody has problems. You can't bring your problems to the ballpark. When you're going through a divorce, just like when I went through my [gambling] investigation, the only time I had control of things was when I was on the field. Because that's the only place everybody leaves you alone. They can't fuck with you because you're on the field. I mean, when you're going through something like that, you wish you could play 23 hours a day."

Rose's focus amazed Luzinski.

"One thing I always said about Pete Rose is whether you liked him or didn't like him, you had to respect him as a player because of one thing: he said things in the clubhouse and went out and did them," he said. "It was unbelievable. He'd tell you, 'I'll get three off him tonight,' or 'I'll get two off him.' And he'd get them, you know?"

Unfortunately for them, former Phillies manager Doc Prothro, who led the Phillies to three-straight 100-loss seasons from 1939 to 1941, died in 1971, so he couldn't be asked about it. Unfortunately for them, Hugh "Losing Pitcher" Mulcahy, who pitched for the Phillies from 1935 to 1940 and 1945 to 1946, died in 2001, so he couldn't be asked about it. That left Utley and Rollins and Howard.

"We've just been in business a long time," Giles said.

That's how most current and former Phillies looked at the milestone. The Phillies have been in business since 1883, so of course they're going to have a lot of losses.

"To me that's a record of nothing but history," said Clay Dalrymple, who caught for the Phillies from 1960 to 1968. "If you look through the history of something like baseball or sporting events, I think you'll find that things even out over time. If you go the next 100 years, maybe it'll be the Dodgers with the worst record and the Phillies with the best. Things have a tendency to level off. Look at the World Series or All-Star Game. One year you look up and see the National League is way ahead of the American League, and then 12 years later the American League has won 10 in a row and they're tied again. Those things have a tendency to even themselves out. I wouldn't be affected by it. I wouldn't even think about it, quite frankly."

If the Dark Ages for the Phillies fell from 1918 to 1949, the Golden Age for the Phillies would be their current 35-year stretch, where their .510 winning percentage is the eighth-best in baseball. They have been to the postseason 10 times from 1976 to 2009. That includes their only two World Series championships in 1980 and 2008, National League pennants in 1983, 1993, and 2009, and National League East championships in 1976, 1977, 1978, and 2007. So players from those great '70s and '80s teams and players from the current team, which hasn't had a losing season since 2002, dismissed the buildup to 10,000 losses as somebody else's problem, not theirs.

"We were more on the winning end of it than the losing end of it," said Greg Luzinski, who played for the Phillies from 1970 to 1980. "When you only have two world championships, it's kind of sad, but I'm close to the Phillies, and I'm close to the owners. Nobody likes losing, no question about it."

"10,000?" said Bob Miller, who pitched for the Phillies from 1949 to 1958 and went 42–42 in his career. "Hell, I only contributed to 42 of those."

The best and worst players in Phillies history played a part in it. Managers made bad moves. General managers made bad trades. Owners pinched their pennies. But it was strange to see fans celebrate defeat so gleefully.

Former Phillies general manager Ed Wade was at the helm when the Phillies developed homegrown talent like Rollins, Utley, Howard, Pat Burrell, Cole Hamels, and Brett Myers. He recalled one day when he was on the concourse at Citizens Bank Park, doing a call-in show with Phillies fans before a game. A woman held up a sign in front of him telling him how close the Phillies were to 10,000 losses.

"To me it was trying to find ways to be miserable," Wade said. "And to have other people be miserable because you want to be. The lady with the sign was baffling to me. The accompanying discussion last season about it was equally as mind-boggling."

It was just one more mind-boggling event in 127 years of sometimes-mind-boggling baseball.

LET THE MAN PITCH

Robin Roberts never considered himself extraordinary, and he still doesn't. He just took the ball and pitched.

He pitched until Phillies managers Ben Chapman, Eddie Sawyer, Steve O'Neill, and Mayo Smith pried the ball from his right hand. But O'Neill, who managed Roberts from 1952 to 1954, never took the ball from Roberts' hand in a remarkable streak of 28 consecutive complete games from August 28, 1952, to July 5, 1953.

"I just kept pitching," Roberts said, sounding completely unimpressed with the feat. "Nobody came out. Some games I'd win 9–7. Once I got into a groove and I was pretty successful at it, well, they just left me in. Steve was an old-timer. He figured if you're getting them out, keep going."

The streak ended July 9, 1953, when O'Neill pulled Roberts in the eighth inning with the Phillies trailing the Brooklyn Dodgers 5–4 at Connie Mack Stadium. The Phillies came back to win 6–5.

Roberts went 21–6 with a 2.50 ERA during the streak with one no-decision that came in a 1–1 five-inning tie against the St. Louis Cardinals on April 30, 1953. In 256 innings, he allowed 232 hits, 45 walks, and 22 home runs. He struck out 130. He threw three shutouts, and opponents hit just .237 against him. He made one relief appearance.

It's a miracle his arm remained attached to his body.

"I had a routine," Roberts explained. "I played a lot of pepper, which they don't play anymore. I ran, although once the season started I didn't run a whole lot. I'd always pitch batting practice between starts. I'd pitch about 10 minutes, just popping it in there. If a guy hit one upstairs I'd throw a little harder the next one, you know? Those are the kind of things you did. You just took care of yourself. And I had a good delivery. Anybody that pitches nine innings, they have a good delivery. And I had one. But in those days I wasn't the only one. There was Warren Spahn

Robin Roberts works out on the mound for his Philadelphia Phillies before a game in 1950.

and Sal Maglie, too. The guys that were pitching regularly on teams, if they got to the seventh inning with a good lead, they left them in there. They figured, hey, they're getting them out."

That doesn't happen today. Consider that from 2004 through 2009, the entire Phillies team had just 29 complete games. Teams today have five-man rotations and typically seven pitchers in their bullpens. Pitch counts are monitored closely. Fans flip out if their ace throws more than 125 pitches. So can front-office officials, who have invested tens of millions of dollars into their ace's arm. Relief pitchers have specific roles, and they're used that way. Three-run lead entering the eighth inning? Bring in the setup man. Still got that lead in the ninth? Bring in the closer.

The game has changed. Roberts' teammate Curt Simmons recalled that, before he joined the Phillies in 1947, his minor-league manager had been instructed not to take him out of the game no matter what. Simmons is certain there were games where he was wild and ineffective and threw 200 or more pitches.

But if you think Roberts is one of those crusty old ballplayers who believe everything from the past is better than the present, think again.

"I think today there are a lot of reasons for doing it," Roberts said, asked why today's pitchers rarely pitch nine innings. "I think sometimes they take out guys that are really in a groove and don't pitch nine innings just because they pitch 100 pitches. But I think overall the approach now is much better all around. They use all the pitchers more. It's more of a team thing, you know, rather than individuals."

But the question remains: how can one man pitch that many innings in that short a span and not feel it in his elbow? His shoulder? His back? His entire body? Oh, Roberts felt it. He just pitched through it.

"I think there were aches and pains in your shoulder or your elbow, and you just assumed after a couple of innings that you'd work it out," Roberts said. "And it did work out that way, the more you got relaxed and loose in the game. I imagine a lot of pitchers have pitched games where they started off with the shoulder not feeling so good, but once you got sweating and into the heat of the game it would come around. I think now there's a tendency of when that happens, pitchers they automatically quit throwing. They say it doesn't feel right. And they're right. It doesn't feel right. I think if they went a little further it might come around. I don't disagree with what they do now. I think they take care of themselves. The club takes care of their pitchers. And they have

WHAT ABOUT NOW, BIG BOY?

Mike Schmidt had suffered enough. Greg Luzinski and Larry Bowa had suffered enough, too.

Pittsburgh Pirates right-hander Bruce Kison had a reputation for coming inside on hitters. Bowa, Schmidt, and Luzinski talked about Kison's reputation during a game on July 8, 1977, at Three Rivers Stadium in Pittsburgh.

"Everybody wanted to go out and get this guy, right?" Schmidt said. "He hit Bull, he hit me, he hit our right-handed hitters. He was a nasty sidearm pitcher. Sooner or later, you've got to say, 'I understand. You want me to be scared up there.' You can hit me once. You can hit me twice. But you can't hit me the third time."

"When Bull got hit and thought someone was throwing at him, he'd go after him," Bowa said. "I remember sitting in the middle of Bull and Schmitty. And Schmitty is bitching about getting hit. And Bull says, 'Damn it, Schmitty, next time you get hit go out there, we'll be behind you. I'm sick of you talking about it.'"

Schmidt had walked in the first inning against Kison. He grounded out in the third and doubled in the sixth. But Kison drilled Schmidt in the middle of the back with a 2–0 fastball in the seventh.

"The thing is, I was hot," said Schmidt, who was hitting .560 [14-for-25] with five home runs and 12 RBIs in his previous eight games. "If you don't think he was trying to hit me, you're crazy. I know for a fact he was trying to hit me."

Schmidt took a couple steps down the first-base line. Should he go after him or should he put his head down and walk to first?

"I didn't really know how to do it," Schmidt said. "I was new at that whole charge-the-mound thing."

So Schmidt pointed at Kison and said, "You throw at me again, I'm coming out there."

"What about now, big boy?" Kison responded.

OK, now. Schmidt charged, and a brawl ensued. And when the bodies had been separated and order had been restored, Schmidt's right ring finger had been broken.

"You don't know what it's like until you're at the bottom of a pile and all you see are Nikes and Adidas and Pumas," Schmidt said. "You don't know whose feet they are. You just know that everybody's feet are everywhere."

Schmidt didn't hit for the next three games, but the finger affected his season. He was hitting .292 with 25 homers and 56 RBIs in 78 games through July 8. He hit .255 with 13 homers and 45 RBIs in the remaining 76 games.

"I said, 'Nice going, Bull,'" Bowa said. "Unbelievable. Bull was getting on him. 'Go out there, goddamn it. Stop talking.' Sure enough he went out there that night, broken finger, out. Yeah, nice advice, Bull."

more pitchers that they use. It's the way it is. As much as you can talk about the old times, it is the new times. And the old-time stuff, it was fun, but it's probably more fun to talk about than it actually was."

It is fun to talk about because Roberts' run is unthinkable today. But as common as complete games were then, Roberts' teammates remain impressed at what he accomplished.

"He was like the old diesel engine. He got better as time went," Simmons said. "He had strong legs and he had the smooth delivery. He had the whole thing. He was the opposite of me. I was herky-jerky and wild. But he could pitch on three days' rest. No problem. He could pitch on the fourth day. Steve O'Neill wanted me to pitch every fourth day, and I did for a couple years, but I came up with a sore arm. I needed a little more time every now and then. But Robbie, he was a real machine, man. He was as tough as they get. I tell the guys I've been lucky. I've played with Roberts and I've played with [Bob] Gibson. Two of the toughest pitchers around, you know? Gibson probably had better stuff, but Robbie would give you a comfortable 0-for-4, you know? He'd throw that fastball. He was tough. He was in the game. He was a real tiger."

Pitching nine innings and pitching on just three days' rest might have been the way they played baseball then, but you still had to endure it. You still had to fight through the discomfort. You had to be tough, and Roberts was one of the toughest.

IT AIN'T OVER 'TIL IT'S OVER

1964

It remains the greatest and arguably most famous collapse in baseball history.

The Phillies had a six-and-a-half-game lead over the St. Louis Cardinals and Cincinnati Reds with 12 games to play on September 20, 1964. They had just beaten the Los Angeles Dodgers on the road and were returning to Philadelphia to open a seven-game homestand at Connie Mack Stadium against the Reds and Milwaukee Braves. Those remaining 12 games were a coronation for the Phillies, who were headed to their first World Series since 1950 and their third World Series in franchise history.

World Series tickets had been printed. Travel plans had been made. The Phillies needed to win just a few more games, except they couldn't. They started an unforgettable 10-game losing streak on September 21 to lose 10 of their remaining 12 games. Meanwhile, the Cardinals went 10–3 in that stretch. The Reds went 9–4.

"People remember that we lost 10 straight games," Cookie Rojas said. "But how come nobody beat them?"

The Cardinals, who finished a game ahead of the Phillies and Reds, couldn't believe their fortune.

"We were trying to finish second because the Phillies were so far in front," said Curt Simmons, who picked up a win against the Phillies on September 30. "We figure there's no way we can catch them because they had a six-and-a-half-game lead. We were trying to do the best we could. The Phillies just collapsed."

"I don't know if that's appropriate wordage—*we came back*," said Tim McCarver, who hit a two-run homer against Jim Bunning in the Cardinals' 8–5 victory September 30. "We ended up winning more games than they did."

It seemed everything that could go wrong went wrong for the Phillies. They couldn't get that big hit, that big out, that big play to snap the streak. Things just kept rolling away from them.

"Things that normally don't happen, happened to us," Johnny Briggs said.

"I always say this and I really truly believe this," Ruben Amaro said. "When the saints that protect in baseball turn around and give you their back, nothing can help you. Nothing. I really, truly believe it. There were so many ridiculous things that happened to us. Too many things. Too many truly curious things."

That curiously painful finish looked like this:

September 21—Chico Ruiz. It's one of the most notorious names in Phillies history. Ruiz, a rookie utility infielder for the Reds, inexplicably stole home with two outs in the top of the sixth inning in a scoreless tie at Connie Mack. And he stole home with Frank Robinson at the plate. Phillies right-hander Art Mahaffey should have had Ruiz out at the plate, but he threw the ball to the backstop to allow Ruiz to score.

"[Reds manager] Dick Sisler said if he wouldn't have scored he would have sent him back to Cuba," Rojas said.

The Reds won 1–0.

"It's one of those things that simply isn't done," Ray Kelly wrote in the *Philadelphia Evening Bulletin*. "Nobody tries to steal home with a slugging great like Frank Robinson at the plate. Not in the sixth inning of a scoreless game."

Nobody does, but Ruiz did. The Reds moved within five and a half games of the Phillies. The Cardinals moved within six games.

"I think it was the beginning of a lot of things," Amaro said.

September 22—Chris Short couldn't get through the fifth inning in a 9–2 loss to the Reds. The Reds moved four and a half games back, and the Cardinals moved five games back.

September 23—The Reds scored four runs in the seventh inning to beat the Phillies 6–4. The Reds moved within three and a half games. The Cardinals remained five back.

September 24—The Phillies opened a four-game series against the Braves, and Wade Blasingame outpitched Jim Bunning in a 5–3 defeat. The Cardinals swept the Pittsburgh Pirates in a doubleheader. The Phillies stood just three ahead of the Reds and three and a half ahead of the Cardinals.

"I remember Bobby Bragan was managing every game for the Braves like it was the last game of the World Series," Briggs said. "Every time, every game he was making all these switches and changes. I remember he wanted to beat us. And they did. They beat us up real bad."

September 25—The Phillies had a 1–0 lead behind Short in the sixth inning, but the Braves took a 3–1 lead in the eighth. Johnny Callison hit a two-run homer in the bottom of the eighth. Joe Torre hit a two-run homer in the tenth to hand the Braves a 5–3 lead, and Dick Allen hit a two-run homer in the bottom of the tenth to keep the Phillies alive. The score remained tied until Phillies pitcher John Boozer allowed two runs in the twelfth inning to take a 7–5 loss. Meanwhile, the Reds swept a doubleheader from the New York Mets to move within one and a half games, and the Cardinals beat the Pirates to move within two and a half games.

September 26—Bobby Shantz had a one-run lead in the top of the ninth inning when everything went haywire. Hank Aaron hit a leadoff single. Eddie Mathews singled to right. Pinch-hitter Frank Bolling hit a ball to Amaro at shortstop. He flipped the ball to Tony Taylor at second base, but Taylor dropped the ball to load the bases with no outs.

Rico Carty tripled to clear the bases to give the Braves a 6–4 lead.

Warren Spahn entered the game and retired the side to pick up the save. It was the Phillies' sixth straight loss. The Reds beat the Mets to move within a half game. And Simmons, who pitched for the Whiz Kids in 1950, led the Cardinals to a victory over the Pirates to move within one and a half games.

September 27—The Phillies finally lost their hold on first place in the National League. They wouldn't get it back.

Bunning was pitching on just two days' rest and had little in the tank in a 14–8 loss to the Braves for their seventh straight loss. It wasted a big game from Callison, who hit three home runs. The Reds swept the Mets in a doubleheader to win their ninth straight game and move into first place with a one-game lead over the Phillies. The Cardinals beat the Pirates to sit one and a half games back of the Reds.

"I'll tell you what bothered me particularly was when we were playing Milwaukee and they just cleaned our clocks big time," Clay Dalrymple said. "I remember they were catching up to beat us, and a ground ball was hit to Tony Taylor for a double play. But the ball hit something in front of him and it bounced straight up in the air and over his head. To me that was like 'Oh, my goodness. God does not want us to win this. He does not want us to win.' To me that's what took the wind out of the sails more than anything else."

September 28—Short pitched on two days' rest and lost 5–1 to Bob Gibson and the St. Louis Cardinals. The Phillies had lost eight straight games. The Reds, who didn't play, held a one-game lead over the Cardinals and a one-and-a-half-game lead over the Phillies.

September 29—Phillies manager Gene Mauch started the ailing Dennis Bennett, who allowed five hits and three runs before he was pulled after just one and a third innings in a 4–2 loss to the Cardinals. Callison, who was terribly sick, asked for his jacket after he hit a pinch-hit single in the seventh. He was so weak that Cardinals first baseman Bill White actually snapped up the buttons for him. The Phillies had lost nine straight. The Reds lost to the Pirates to put them in a first-place tie with the Cardinals. The Phillies were one and a half games back.

"Dennis Bennett had a bad arm," Simmons said. "He shouldn't have even been pitching. We knocked the heck out of him. Mauch had other guys to pitch. I don't know why he did that. He was just kind of goosing it up there because he had a bad arm."

Phillies manager Gene Mauch shouts as he bats the ball and directs the fielding practice for pitchers at the opening of Phillies spring training on February 29, 1964, in Clearwater, Florida. Photo courtesy of AP Images.

September 30—Bunning pitched on just two days' rest again and lost 8–5 to the Cardinals. The Phillies had lost 10 straight, while the Cardinals had won eight straight. The Reds had lost 1–0 in 16 innings at home to the Pirates to move the Cardinals into first place. The Reds sat a game back, while the Phillies were two and a half games back with just two games to play.

October 2—The Reds had beaten the Pirates a day earlier to move within a half-game of the Cardinals, with the Phillies in town for a two-game series to finish the season. The Phillies needed to sweep the Reds on the road, and the Cardinals needed to lose three straight to the lowly Mets, who were 51–108 and the worst team in baseball.

Short, pitching on three days' rest, allowed just one earned run in six and a third innings. But the Phillies trailed 3–0 entering the top of the eighth inning when Frank Thomas hit a one-out single, Rojas walked, and Taylor singled to center to score the Phillies' first run. Callison struck out for the second out, but Allen tripled to score Rojas and Taylor to tie it. Alex Johnson singled to score Allen to give the Phillies a 4–3 victory and snap their 10-game losing streak.

Incredibly, Mets left-hander Al Jackson outpitched Cardinals ace Bob Gibson in a 1–0 victory. The Cardinals maintained a half-game lead over the Reds, and the Phillies sat one and a half games back.

October 3—The Reds and Phillies had the day off, but both enjoyed the fact that the Mets beat the Cardinals again. This time it moved the Cardinals and Reds into a first-place tie and the Phillies one game back with one to play.

October 4—The Phillies entered the final game of the season needing to beat the Reds and for the Mets to beat the Cardinals to force a three-way tie for the pennant. Bunning threw a shutout in a 10–0 victory over the Reds. But the Cardinals beat the Mets 11–5 to clinch the pennant.

The Phillies had blown it.

Mauch had pitched Bunning and Short, each on two days' rest twice, in those final 12 games. Mauch has been second-guessed ever since.

"You could see the frustration on his face because he just wanted to win one game," Briggs said.

But the players still find it difficult to blame Mauch for the collapse.

"When my time comes and I go wherever Gene Mauch is, I'm going to go play for him," Amaro said. "I think that you can go ahead and blame it on the manager if you want to, but the guys that actually perform were us on the field. And we had a chance to do it on the field."

THE TEAM TO BEAT

The Phillies' rotten luck finally turned in 2007.

They would not choke away an insurmountable lead like they had in 1964. They would not fall short like they had in 2003, when they held the National League wild-card lead with eight games to play only to finish 1–7. Or 2005, when they finished the season 14–6 only to fall a game behind the Houston Astros for the wild card. Or 2006, when they held the wild-card lead with seven games to play only to finish 3–4.

Close calls and near misses. Not this time.

Jimmy Rollins boldly proclaimed the Phillies the team to beat before the 2007 season, and this time it actually came true. The Phillies were seven games behind the New York Mets in the National League East on September 12, 2007, with just 17 games to play. The East was a long shot, and players in the Phillies clubhouse knew it. They figured at this point they should just forget about the Mets and focus on the wild card.

"There's no sense in me sugarcoating it," Charlie Manuel said after a 12–0 loss to the Colorado Rockies dropped them seven back with 17 to play. "It's kind of a 'show me' time. It's kind of like, 'Let's go. If we have it, let's see it.' That's kind of how I look at it. We've got 17 games left. That's what it's come down to. It's no time to talk. Let's do it."

Then the miracle happened. The Phillies won 13 of their remaining 17 games, while the Mets went into an epic freefall, losing 12 of their remaining 17 to hand the Phillies their first NL East championship since 1993.

September 13—The Phillies beat the Colorado Rockies 12–4 in a series finale at Citizens Bank Park. Manuel pulled righthander J.D. Durbin after he allowed five hits and three runs in just one inning. Geoff Geary, Clay Condrey, Kane Davis, Antonio Alfonseca, J.C. Romero, and Jose Mesa allowed just one run the rest of the way. Their thoughts immediately turned to their upcoming series at Shea Stadium against the Mets, who held a six-and-a-half-game lead over the Phillies.

"It's a big series," Wes Helms said. "Even though the Mets have a big lead, they're going to be gunning for us."

September 14—The Phillies started the Mets on their freefall to oblivion with a 3–2 victory in 10 innings. Greg Dobbs' sacrifice fly scored Jayson Werth to win it. It moved the Phillies within five and a half games of first place.

"I can't," said Manuel, when asked to explain his team's sixth straight victory over the Mets. "We've played them good. We're going to make it seven tomorrow. Get Pedro [Martinez] tomorrow. I have had a lot of losses with Pedro pitching. We're due to get some."

September 15—Jimmy Rollins hit a ball over Mets center fielder Carlos Beltran's head in the eighth inning to score two runs in a 5–3 victory to move the Phillies within four and a half games of first place.

"Anytime we're down two or three runs, I start stretching," closer Brett Myers said. "I get a good feeling."

September 16—The Phillies beat the Mets 10–6, highlighted by Dobbs' pinch-hit grand slam in the sixth inning. The sweep was complete, and the Mets, who had lost eight straight games to the Phillies, were wondering what the heck happened as their lead shrunk to just three and a half games.

"I don't know if we're in their heads, but I think we've proven to them that we can play them tough," Dobbs said.

September 17—The Phillies carried an 11–0 lead into the bottom of the sixth inning against the St. Louis Cardinals at Busch Stadium but survived 13–11. The Mets lost 12–4 to the Washington Nationals at RFK Stadium to cut their lead to two and a half games.

"It was trying my heart," Manuel said. "It was starting to beat a little bit quick. That's all right. That's a good test for it, I guess. It was unreal. I will have some VO tonight when I get back to my room."

September 18—In a sign that nothing is easy, the Phillies beat the Cardinals 7–4 in 14 innings. Myers blew a one-run lead in the tenth to extend the game an extra four innings, but catcher Rod Barajas, who fell out of favor with fans earlier in the season after he allowed a runner to slide between his legs to score in Florida, got the game-winning hit in the fourteenth. The Mets lost 9–8 to the Nationals, to cut their lead to one and a half games.

"They're coming this way, and we're going that way," Manuel said of the Mets. "And that's good. We'll leave it there. If they keep coming this way, we'll catch them."

September 19—The Phillies lost a game in the standings to the Mets after a 2–1 loss to the Cardinals in 10 innings. The Mets beat the Nationals 8–4.

"Why not?" Myers said, when told it would be unrealistic to think the Phillies could keep winning and the Mets could keep losing. "Why not? You've seen teams blow 10-game leads before, haven't you? I think this is one of the teams that did do it a long time ago. It can happen."

September 20—The Phillies trailed the Nationals by four runs entering the seventh inning at RFK but scored four in the seventh and one run in the eighth in a 7–6 victory. Werth hit a three-run homer in the seventh. Rollins doubled to score the winning run in the eighth.

"We've still got some games to play," Werth said. "We're right where we need to be."

That's because the Mets lost to the Florida Marlins 8–7 at Dolphin Stadium in 10 innings, to trim their lead to one and a half games. Jorge Sosa blew a three-run lead in the ninth because Mets closer Billy Wagner was unavailable with back spasms.

"A lot of crazy stuff is happening," Tom Glavine said. "Some of it, you can't believe. We've lost every which way. It's hard to believe it's happening."

September 21—Adam Eaton had pitched terribly for most of the season but allowed three runs in five innings in a 6–3 victory over the Nationals. The Mets beat the Marlins 9–6 to maintain their one-and-a-half-game lead.

"We're playing loose and free," Eaton said. "We're just on a roll at the right time."

September 22—The Phillies scored three runs in the tenth inning in a 4–1 victory over the Nationals. Romero, Tom Gordon, and Myers each pitched for the fifth consecutive day to preserve the win. The Mets beat the Marlins 7–2 to remain one and a half games up.

"That's why you work in the off-season," Romero said. "In the off-season, you train for this moment. Right now, it's the time of year where your teammates need you. They're counting on you."

Brett Myers celebrates after striking out Willie Mo Pena of the Washington Nationals, giving the Phillies the divisional championship at Citizens Bank Park on September 30, 2007.

September 23—The Phillies had a one-run lead entering the bottom of the sixth but couldn't hold it in a 5–3 loss to the Nationals. The Mets beat the Marlins 7–6 in 11 innings to take a two-and-a-half-game lead.

"We definitely have to have a big homestand," Manuel said. Daunting?

"Why would it be?" Aaron Rowand said. "It's exciting. Glass is half full, pal. It's not half empty."

September 24—The Mets lost 13–4 to the Nationals at Shea. Their lead was down to two with six to play.

September 25—The Braves scored six runs in five and a third innings against Jamie Moyer in a 10–6 victory over the Phillies. The Mets lost 10–9 to the Nationals.

"You look up there [at the scoreboard], and you see the Mets losing," Manuel said. "It's sitting right there in front of you."

September 26—Kyle Lohse allowed two runs in seven innings as the Phillies moved within a game of the Mets with four games to play. The Mets lost 9–6 to the Nationals.

"OK," Myers said. "Now it's really time to take care of business. I just want to see that upper deck full tomorrow. I want so many people here that I can't even get home because of the traffic. I think that's what we all want to see. I know it's a school night, but come on. Let's go. Let's get it done."

September 27—The Phillies scored four runs in the first inning off John Smoltz in a 6–4 victory that put the Phillies into a first-place tie with the Mets with just three games to play. St. Louis Cardinals right-hander Joel Pineiro threw eight shutout innings in a 3–0 victory over the Mets.

"We're still going to win this thing. We're still going to win it," Mets manager Willie Randolph said as he walked through the Mets' clubhouse.

A 162-game season suddenly came down to the final weekend.

"It is crazy," Rollins said. "It is. It definitely is. You'd like for things to be easier. Who wouldn't like for things to be easier? But sports wouldn't be as fun if it was that way."

"It's got to be like that, right?" Chase Utley said. "That's what makes it exciting. That's what you train in the off-season for. You come to spring training with your goal to be in this situation at the end of the year."

September 28—Cole Hamels threw eight shutout innings in a 6–0 victory over the Nationals. The Mets lost 7–4 to the Marlins, to put the Phillies in sole possession of first place for the first time this season.

"It's not Sunday," Gordon said. "When you see that plastic up [to cover the clubhouse lockers for a celebration], then you'll know what time it is."

"I'm embarrassed," Mets third baseman David Wright said. "I think it's embarrassing. It's pretty pathetic that we have the division in our grasp with seven home games, and we can't find a way to win one of them. It's a bad feeling."

September 29—Eaton lasted only two and a third innings as the Nationals beat the Phillies 4–2 to put the Phillies back into a first-place tie with the Mets heading into the final game of the season. The Mets beat the Marlins 13–0.

"We've been eliminated a couple of times on the last day," Rollins said. "Why not break through on the last day? Nothing has been easy all year long, so we shouldn't expect it to be easy at the end."

"It's bizarre, really," Randolph said. "This whole month has been bizarre."

September 30—In a game few will forget, Moyer allowed one unearned run in five and a third innings in a 6–1 victory over the Nationals. The Mets lost 8–1 to the Marlins as the Phillies captured their first NL East championship since 1993.

Rollins was right. The Phillies were the team to beat.

"It was all on us," Rollins said. "We had the chemistry. We had the makeup. We had the talent. We had a beautiful park to do it in. But something was missing, and that was winning that big game on the last day of the season."

GEE WHIZ, WHAT'S HAPPENING?

The losing became too much to bear, so Curt Simmons turned off the radio and stopped listening.

Simmons had been on pace to win 20-plus games for the Phillies in 1950, but he left the team September 10 when his National Guard unit—the 20th Infantry Division—was activated as the Korean War escalated. Simmons, who followed the action the rest of the season on the radio, had signed up for the National Guard in 1948 at the request of Phillies owner Bob Carpenter, who thought it would be a way for Simmons to beat the peacetime draft.

"It was tough," Simmons said. "But it wasn't a sudden thing. It was something that was developing."

Simmons had attended training for a few days in August in Indiantown Gap, Pennsylvania. He knew then he probably would not finish the season with the Whiz Kids when an officer told the group of men there, "You've got 30 days. Go home and get your affairs in order. You're going to be in the army."

Simmons entered the army on September 5 but stayed in the armory on Broad and Diamond Streets in North Philadelphia for the next few days. He would be in the armory from 7:00 AM to 5:00 PM and then join the Phillies at night. He started but wasn't involved in the decision as the Phillies lost to the Brooklyn Dodgers 3–2 in the second game of a doubleheader on September 6. He pitched again on September 9, helping beat the Boston Braves 7–6. Simmons hopped on a train the next morning for Camp Attebury in Indiana. He wouldn't return.

"It was tough because we were rolling, and I was having a good year," Simmons said. "Everybody was doing well. They kept telling me, 'We're going to get you back.' I said, 'Good luck, I hope so.' But nothing ever happened."

The Phillies tried to get Simmons a 30-day extension so he could finish the season with the team and presumably help them play in their first World Series since 1915.

"I was getting on a train, and the traveling secretary said we'll get you back, and I said, 'Yeah, we'll see,'" Simmons said. "They tried, but they weren't letting anybody out. The war was on."

It was on for the Phillies, too. They lost two more starters in the next six days. They lost rookie right-hander Bubba Church on September 15, when Cincinnati Reds first baseman Ted Kluszewski crushed a line drive off his face. They lost rookie right-hander Bob Miller the next day with a sore right shoulder.

"I thought he was dead," Miller said about Church. "It was a terrific line drive. It was a low fastball, and Ted Kluszewski hit it like a two-iron right in his eye. Woo. I saw him get hit, and he put his hands up to his face and went down on his knees. He moved his hands away when he got down, and I said, 'Oh my God, it's World War II all over again.' He got hit. I mean, it was that vicious. It was that bad. That killed him. Absolutely."

Miller's shoulder problems came from a freak injury in late June, when he tripped on some steps at a North Philadelphia train station and threw out his back. He came back too early from the injury and subsequently injured his shoulder. He had been 8–0 when he fell. He finished 11–6.

"I went out to pitch the seventh inning [against the Reds on September 16], and holy geez, I had a lot of pain in my right shoulder," he said.

There were other injuries, too. Bill Nicholson was lost for the season because of diabetes. Right fielder Dick Sisler had been fighting a sore left wrist for weeks. Catcher Andy Seminick broke his ankle on a play at the plate September 27 but shot up the ankle with painkillers and finished the season.

But the injuries took their toll. The Phillies were 86–54 with a seven-and-a-half-game lead over the Brooklyn Dodgers in the National League on September 16, the day they lost Miller. But because of the losses and injuries to Simmons, Church, Miller, and others, the Phillies lost nine of their next 13 games. The Dodgers went 13–5 to pull within a game of the Phillies with one game to play.

"We were losing games on goofy stuff," Simmons said. "We were making errors. We were hanging by a thread."

"We were hurting," catcher Stan Lopata said.

So it came down to that final game. The Phillies win, they win their first pennant since 1915. They lose, they have a three-game playoff against the Dodgers. Nobody on the Phillies wanted that.

"I didn't even want to listen," Simmons said. "They kept losing down the stretch there. I said, 'Geez, I'm not going to listen to this.' I'll go out with the guys. I was out playing touch football with some guys between the barracks."

That's when he heard the good news.

"Sisler hit a home run! You guys are winning!"

Sisler had hit a three-run homer in the top of the tenth inning to beat the Dodgers 4–1. The Phillies had survived.

"We had some kind of great attitude on that ballclub that somebody was always going to pick somebody up," Miller said. "We just had that can't-lose attitude. I've never been on another club like it. Unbelievable."

THE DREAM TEAM: THE PLAYERS

There are 10 players in the National Baseball Hall of Fame and Museum in Cooperstown, New York, who played primarily for the Phillies: pitcher Grover Cleveland Alexander, center fielder Richie Ashburn, shortstop Dave Bancroft, pitcher Steve Carlton, left fielder Ed Delahanty, center fielder Billy Hamilton, right fielder Chuck Klein, pitcher Robin Roberts, third baseman Mike Schmidt, and right fielder Sam Thompson.

Only Alexander, Ashburn, Carlton, Roberts, and Schmidt make this Phillies Dream Team.

No Delahanty. No Hamilton. No Klein.

Crazy? No, not really.

Delahanty's .346 career average is the fifth-best in baseball history. Hamilton's .344 average is tied with Ted Williams for seventh-best all-time. Klein won the Triple Crown in 1933 and arguably had the most dominating first five seasons of any player in history.

But baseball before 1900 was a much different game than it is today. The number of balls required for a walk went from eight in 1880 to four in 1889, with increases and decreases in between. The pitcher's mound only moved to 60'6" in 1893. Rules constantly seemed to be changing. In the 1890s first basemen regularly grabbed the belts of base-runners to prevent them from running around the bases. If that didn't work, base-runners were tripped or pushed. It was the Wild West on a diamond. Fights happened regularly. Umpires were abused. So with all due respect to Delahanty, Hamilton, and Thompson—they were the first and only outfield in baseball history to hit .400 or better in 1894—they're out. It's simply impossible to compare their era to the post-1900 modern era. And Klein? He never would have been in the Hall of Fame if he hadn't played at Baker Bowl, which skewed his numbers with its short porch in right field. As Jayson Stark wrote in *The Stark Truth*, "All those early stats come attached to a gigantic asterisk: *Got to play in Baker Bowl.*"

So how did we come up with this team?

First, we sought the opinions of countless baseball people, folks who have spent their lives in the game and have seen these players play. There were some easy choices, where we didn't need much help. Nobody argued with Schmidt at third base, Chase Utley at second base, or Jimmy Rollins at shortstop. Others were trickier. Bob Boone or Darren Daulton behind the plate? Bobby Abreu, Johnny Callison, or Klein in right field? Lenny Dykstra or Ashburn in center field? Ryan Howard or Pete Rose at first base? The baseball lifers made strong cases all around the diamond, and we listened intently to each one.

Second, we considered each player's career with the Phillies—and only his career with the Phillies. Dick Allen is a perfect example. We threw out his years with the St. Louis Cardinals, Los Angeles Dodgers, and Chicago White Sox, where he won the American League MVP in 1972. We also considered his time as a third baseman separately from his time as a first baseman. Allen played 545 games at third base and 315 games at first base for the Phillies. If we added those numbers together, Allen's statistics could make a winning case for being the Dream Team's first baseman. But because he put up his best numbers at third base—and we separated his offensive production at third from his offensive production at first—he does not. Not everybody agreed with that thinking.

"If Dick Allen played one game at first base, that should be enough to put him there," former Phillies manager Jim Fregosi said.

THE CHAMP IS HERE

Five Phillies have won batting titles in the National League:
- Sherry Magee in 1910 (.331).
- Lefty O'Doul in 1929 (.398).
- Chuck Klein in 1933 (.368).
- Richie Ashburn in 1955 (.338).
- Richie Ashburn in 1958 (.350).

But we did it that way because that's how baseball recognizes its records. Mike Piazza hit 427 home runs in his career, but when you look at the record book for most home runs in baseball history for a catcher, he has 396. That's because he hit 31 of his homers as a designated hitter (18), first baseman (eight), and pinch-hitter (five).

Third, we looked at the numbers. While it is obviously difficult to compare eras, there is a way to show how much a player produced offensively in his era compared to other players in their eras. Sabermetrician Lee Sinins has two statistics: Runs Created Above Average (RCAA) and Runs Created Above Average at his Position (RCAP). Runs created (RC) is a statistic Moneyball inspiration Bill James developed to project how many runs a player creates over the course of a season or career. Sinins uses RCAA to determine the difference between a player's RC total and the total for an average player who used the same amount of his team's outs.

RCAP is just like RCAA, except it compares players at the same position.

For example, Rollins finished the 2009 season with a career 28 RCAA, which means he created 28 runs more than the average player over his career. But Rollins also had a 152 RCAP, which means he created 152 more runs than the average shortstop in his career. Compared to other shortstops, Rollins is one of the best. Meanwhile, Larry Bowa had a 19 RCAP over his career, meaning

Rollins outproduced shortstops in his era more than Bowa outproduced shortstops in his.

Lastly, when it came to picking this team, we used our gut.

We're certain there will be disagreements with this team. Everybody has their favorites. Everybody has his opinion. Everybody looks at the same statistics in different ways. But we'll try to make the best case possible for why the following eight position players, five starting pitchers, and one closer are the best at their positions in Phillies history.

Catcher
Bob Boone
1972–81

Defense or offense? Longevity or a flash of brilliance?

Those questions made catcher one of the most difficult positions to choose, because when we're talking about the greatest catchers in Phillies history, we're talking about Bob Boone and Darren Daulton, and they couldn't make more different cases for themselves.

Boone played 10 years for the Phillies, winning two Gold Gloves. He would have won more, except Johnny Bench won 10 consecutive Gold Gloves from 1968 to 1977. Boone actually ended up winning seven Gold Gloves in his career, the third most in baseball history behind Ivan Rodriguez (13) and Bench (10). One wonders how many Boone would have won if he hadn't played in the same era and same league as arguably the greatest catcher in baseball history.

Daulton played parts of 14 seasons with the Phillies from 1983 to 1997 and led the National League with 109 RBIs in 1992. He is one of just four catchers in history to lead their league in RBIs. The other three are in the Hall of Fame: Roy Campanella (1953), Gary Carter (1984), and Bench (1970, 1972, and 1974). But knee injuries limited much of Daulton's career, which had to be considered.

Bill James ranked Boone the 21st greatest catcher in history in *The Bill James Historical Baseball Abstract* solely because of his defense.

Bob Boone poses for a team portrait. Boone played for the Phillies from 1972 to 1981 and would be part of the all-time Phillies Dream Team.

"A very smart receiver, and worked [as] hard to stay in shape as anyone who ever played baseball," James wrote. "Not much of a hitter, but one of the five greatest defensive catchers of all time."

James ranked Daulton 25th.

"In his career he grounded into only one double play for every 104 at-bats—the best GIDP rate in history for a catcher (since they began keeping GIDP totals, in the 1930s)," James wrote, "and one of the lowest ever. Richie Ashburn grounded into double plays more often, and he was a left-handed leadoff man who could fly."

Daulton had a .908 on-base-plus-slugging percentage in '92, when he hit .270 with 27 homers and 109 RBIs. Boone never sniffed those numbers. He had a career-high .789 OPS in 1979, when he hit .286 with nine homers and 58 RBIs.

Offensively, it's not a contest. But Boone edged Daulton because what a catcher brings behind the plate means a lot to a team's success. Boone also had the more durable career.

"Boonie really had no peer," former Phillies manager Dallas Green said. "What separated Boonie was how he handled the pitching staff. He couldn't hit a lick. He had an awful year in 1980, but I still counted on him to handle my pitching staff. He put the numbers down as good as anybody you'd want to see. And he made the pitchers pitch a game that sometimes they didn't believe in. He did his homework. Daulton's bag is leadership, but Boonie didn't take a backseat to leadership because of his handling of the pitching staff. Offensively, there's no contest with Dutch. But it's still a team game."

Green obviously is biased toward Boone, just like former Phillies manager Jim Fregosi is biased toward Daulton.

"Talentwise, Boonie played on much better teams, which allowed him to be able to just catch and play defense and not swing the bat," Fregosi said. "But Dutch didn't just catch every day. He also hit fourth in the lineup and had to carry the offense. Longevity and careerwise, there's no question Boone had a better career. But in a short period of time, Dutch was the guy. I'd take Dutch because of his leadership qualities and the offensive player he became."

Daulton had a 195 RCAP, meaning he created 195 more runs than the average catcher during his Phillies career. Boone had a horrible -17 RCAP, with his 1980–81 seasons killing his average. But Boone still ranks third amongst Phillies catchers in hits (957); fourth in doubles (172), extra-base hits (258), and RBIs (456); sixth in home runs (65) and runs (349); and ninth in average (.259). Daulton ranks first in walks (546), RCAA (90), and RCAP (160); second in home runs (123) and extra-base hits (316); third in doubles (176) and RBIs (525); sixth in hits (785) and OPS (.777); seventh in SLG (.423); and eighth in OBP (.354).

"You need a catcher that is a catcher first," said Ruben Amaro Sr., who was a coach on the 1980 team. "Bobby Boone remembered the things he had to do with the pitchers. I don't think there was anybody better than him, more consistent. Somebody that stayed in the game. Somebody reliable. Someone that was there. Injuries, nagging injuries, that didn't deter him behind the plate. Taking care of young pitchers, he was outstanding. I know Daulton was an offensive player. Kind of like Mike Piazza, maybe with a little better arm than Piazza. But as far as catching with Boone, there's no comparison. I think Bobby Boone was far better than anybody behind the plate."

First Base
Ryan Howard
2004–Present

To say anybody really knew Ryan Howard would be one of the purest power hitters in baseball is a stretch.

But no player in history has hit 200 home runs faster than Howard. No player has reached 600 RBIs faster since Ted Williams in 1946. Howard is one of just four players in history to win his league's Rookie of the Year and MVP Awards in his first two seasons: Fred Lynn (1975) and Ichiro Suzuki (2001) won both awards in their first years, while Cal Ripken Jr. (1982–83) and Howard won both awards in consecutive years. Howard was National League Rookie of the Year in 2005 and MVP in 2006.

"I'm not a home-run hitter," Ken Griffey Jr. said. "He's a home-run hitter."

Howard is the greatest first baseman in Phillies history, even after playing just a little more than four and a half full seasons in the majors. Pete Rose (1979–83) played an integral part in helping the Phillies win their first World Series championship in 1980, but his numbers don't stack up coming at the end of a Hall of Fame–type career. John Kruk (1989–94) remains a fan favorite and had some impressive seasons, but his numbers don't compare. Other first basemen like Fred Luderus (1910–20), Dolph Camilli (1934–37), and Thome (2003–05) had nice careers with the Phillies, but they never had the impact that Howard has made in such a short period of time.

Howard finished the 2009 season the franchise's leader in home runs for first basemen, with 216. Among first basemen with at least 2,000 plate appearances, he ranked first in on-base-plus-slugging percentage (.958), slugging percentage (.582), RCAA (194), and RCAP (111). He ranked second in RBIs (624) and extra-base hits (358), fourth in on-base percentage (.376), sixth in hits (734) and doubles (131), and seventh in average (.278).

"He's a big man with a lot of pop," Griffey said. "There isn't a ballpark that can hold him."

Before the Phillies traded Jim Thome to the White Sox for Aaron Rowand and a couple pitching prospects in November 2005, the Phillies floated Howard's name to a few teams. It's not that the Phillies wanted to trade Howard, but Thome was a major roadblock in front of him. Thome had signed a six-year, $85 million contract with the Phillies before the 2003 season. Trading him wouldn't be easy.

That was why the Phillies tried Howard in the outfield in spring training in 2005. They wanted to give themselves the chance of having both Howard and Thome in their lineup.

"The feedback was grim," said Ed Wade, the team's general manager. "There wasn't anybody saying, 'Well, maybe.' It was, 'No, it's not going to work.' It was like moving Chase [Utley] to third at one point in time and moving [Pat] Burrell to first before he moved to the outfield. If you don't try those things based on the composition of your club, then you're being shortsighted. At least try. Don't dismiss it out of hand."

The outfield experiment failed, which meant the Phillies had two options: trade Howard or trade Thome. It would be easier to trade Howard because he was young and inexpensive, and other teams would have him under their control for years. But the Phillies weren't going to just give him away. Not that the market for Howard was hot. Howard put up some remarkable numbers in the minor leagues. He hit .304 with 23 home runs and 82 RBIs for Single A Clearwater in 2003. He hit .297 with 37 home runs and 102 RBIs in 102 games for Double A Reading in 2004. But could that translate to the big leagues? Some were skeptical.

"He's hit a lot of home runs in Double A," one general manager told Wade. "But remember Sam Horn."

Wade shook his head.

"He couldn't wait to get off the phone with me," he said.

Horn was a can't-miss prospect for the Boston Red Sox, who never lived up to his hype. Most general managers weren't that frank when they talked with Wade, but they certainly weren't lining up to take Howard off his hands, either. Teams simply weren't going to give up a front-line starting pitcher or even a comparable top prospect for Howard.

"There weren't a lot of front-burner trade discussions involving Ryan," Wade said. "But it would be disingenuous to say that we anticipated everything that happened. That Thome was going to get hurt in 2005, for instance. Because realistically our expectation at that point was that Jim was going to be the face of the franchise for a number of years. He was a premier power guy in our league. People sort of quickly forgot that the acquisition of Jim meant a lot to our franchise in the anticipation of going into Citizens Bank Park. So to say that I envisioned this playing out the way that it did, it wouldn't be true. I guess I envisioned that Jim would continue to be a great player and that at some point in time we would have to make the decision on what was best for the organization in a trade environment with Ryan."

But because Thome got hurt in 2005 and missed the second half of the season, Howard was forced into the lineup. He hit .288 with 22 homers and 63 RBIs in just 88 games. He hit 10 homers in September, the most for a rookie in baseball history. He looked capable of living up to the hype. And that made the trade talk more of a hot-button issue in Philadelphia. Something had to be done. After the Phillies fired Wade and hired Pat Gillick, they shopped both Howard and Thome, with the Pittsburgh Pirates shooting down talks about a potential Howard swap for Zack Duke or Oliver Perez. Thome, who, like Howard, had tired of the speculation about their futures, gave the Phillies a few teams he would play for: the Cleveland Indians, Chicago Cubs, and Chicago White Sox. Thome went to the White Sox and Howard hit .313 with 58 home runs and 149 RBIs in 2006. He set a big-league record for most homers for a player in his sophomore season and a NL record for most RBIs for a player in his sophomore year. He led baseball in homers, RBIs, total bases (383), home-run ratio (10.02), and times on base (299). And for those

BOWA'S INTENSITY

Phillies fans still love Larry Bowa. He hasn't played for the Phillies since 1981. He hasn't managed for the Phillies since 2004. But he is cheered and revered because few players cared as much as he cared.

Greg Luzinski roomed with Bowa on the road, and vividly remembers Bowa's intensity. He remembers an August 30, 1972, game in Houston, where Bowa struck out in the third inning. He was ejected for arguing the call, and became so upset at the ejection that he wouldn't move. Phillies manager Paul Owens told Don Money, who was on deck, to retrieve Bowa, who appeared catatonic in the batter's box. Money knew better, so he looked at Luzinski, Bowa's friend and roommate, and said to Ozark, "Tell him to go get him."

"It's between two to three minutes," Luzinski said. "Bowa hadn't moved. He's frozen. He's standing like a statue at home plate. He's already been kicked out of the game by the umpire. He's trying to get him out of the batter's box, but he doesn't want to touch him obviously. So he's just standing there."

Luzinski bravely left the dugout to retrieve his friend.

"As I went up there to go get him, he turned around and he takes the bat like he's going to swing at me," he said. "I put mine up there to block it."

Bowa finally left the field and returned to the visitor's clubhouse at the Astrodome.

"In Houston, when you went into the dugout you went down a tunnel, up steps, it was a long way to the clubhouse," Luzinski said. "They used to have these little lightbulbs. Well, the game ended and all the lightbulbs were broke. We were feeling the walls. You would go from the bright spots to the dark spots."

It was a long, dark journey back to the clubhouse.

Later, Luzinski and Bowa heard a knock at their hotel room door.

It was Phillies trainer Don Seger.

"Do you mind going downstairs?" Seger said to Luzinski. "I'd like to talk to Larry."

"Sure," Luzinski said.

> Luzinski went to the hotel bar to have a beer. He returned a short time later.
>
> "Can you believe what he said to me?" Bowa said. "He asked me if it ever got so bad that I thought about jumping!"
>
> Bowa hated to lose. It made him miserable. But he wasn't suicidal. Still, from that point on Bowa and Luzinski roomed on the second or third floor in the team hotels. No exceptions.
>
> "We never got higher," Luzinski said laughing. "We could be in a 40-story hotel and we were on the second floor. He was a dandy."

who thought Howard was a beneficiary of playing at cozy Citizens Bank Park, think again. He hit .309 with 29 homers and 75 RBIs in 79 games at home and .318 with 29 homers and 74 RBIs in 80 games on the road.

"He's an unbelievable talent," Rowand said. "He's got ridiculous talent. He's an Alex Rodriguez, Albert Pujols, Big Papi. Those type[s] of guys that can that can literally carry a team by themselves when they get hot."

Second Base
Chase Utley
2003–Present

Few players work harder than Chase Utley.

He typically shows up at the ballpark no later than 1:00 PM for a 7:00 PM game. If it's the first game of a series, he will watch roughly two hours of video. He will study that night's starting pitcher and the relief pitchers he might face. He looks at how those pitchers have pitched him in the past. He looks at how those pitchers have pitched to other left-handed hitters. He watches those at-bats closely, looking for clues, looking for patterns, looking for any details that might help him once he's standing inside the batter's box.

"That's the first day," Phillies team video coordinator Kevin Camiscioli said. "Then the second and third day, it's basically all of his at-bats, other lefties' at-bats of guys on our team. I'm not always sure what he's looking for, but it seems to be working."

It certainly is. Utley, who is the greatest second baseman in Phillies history, signed a seven-year, $85 million contract extension with the Phillies before the 2007 season, and when it finally expires after 2013, it might be considered one of the greatest bargains in baseball. Imagine that: an $85 million bargain. But the consensus from statisticians to scouts is that Utley already is better than former Phillies second basemen like Nap Lajoie, who is in the Hall of Fame. He is better than Juan Samuel. Better than Tony Taylor. Better than Manny Trillo.

"I agree," said Samuel, who played for the Phillies from 1983 to 1989. "It's not even close."

In fact, should Utley remain healthy and productive throughout the remainder of his contract, he should put up numbers so impressive that Phillies fans will be asking if Utley is one of the greatest second basemen in baseball history. Utley finished 2009 first among Phillies second basemen with 2,000 or more plate appearances, in home runs (151), on-base percentage (.383), slugging percentage (.529), on-base-plus-slugging percentage (.912), RCAA (211), RCAP (241), extra-base hits (395), and RBIs (561); second in runs (583); and third in hits (947).

"What impresses me the most is that the kid is very, very solid," said Samuel, whom the Phillies inducted onto their Wall of Fame in 2008. "What a beautiful swing. My goodness. That type of swing stays with you forever. It's just so compact, short, and quick. It's very compact. It's not long at all for somebody who hits home runs. He stays with the ball as long as he can."

That's the talent in Utley coming through. You have to be born with remarkable talent to swing a bat like that.

"He's a great hitter," Phillies hitting coach Milt Thompson said. "You can analyze everything, but the bottom line is that the kid is just an unbelievable hitter. That's what it boils down to. He studies and stuff, but he's just a great talent. He just loves to hit, which is a good thing. When you love to hit and know how to hit, it makes it very simple."

Utley displayed a love for hitting at an early age. He spent hours as a kid at the Lakewood Batting Cages, which is located near the Utley family home in Long Beach, California. Utley's

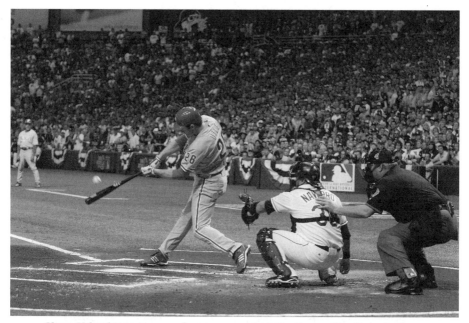

Chase Utley hits a two-run home run against the Tampa Bay Rays during Game 1 of the 2008 World Series on October 22, 2008, at Tropicana Field in St. Petersburg, Florida.

father, Dave, would hand his son a $20 bill and tell him to call when he was finished. He waited hours for that call, and sometimes it never came. One day he drove to the batting cages to find Chase picking up balls, serving hot dogs, doing anything he could for a few extra hacks in the cage. Utley doesn't have to serve hot dogs anymore to get a few extra swings, although he probably would if he had to. He loves to hit, and he gets to the ballpark early every day because he is constantly working on perfecting his swing.

"He studies and prepares for the game as much or more than any other hitter I've been around," Phillies manager Charlie Manuel said. "He's off the charts with preparation. He has a tremendous memory. He's totally ready when the game starts. You'll never catch him not prepared. He knows all about the pitchers. He knows what they want to do. He'll say stuff during the game in the dugout, like when a pitcher comes in. He'll say what he throws and what tendencies that he has. He's the one I notice. Those guys will be asking him."

Why study so much?

"You try to find tendencies," Utley said. "You try to figure out what approach he's going to take to you. Sometimes you're right. Sometimes you're wrong. There are plenty of times when you're wrong. Sometimes it's a huge advantage. There are other times it can mess you up a little bit. But that's the chance you take. But I think video is a huge advantage, especially against the guys you've never faced before. It helps you get an idea of what it might look like. Every pitcher is a little different. Why would you not want to watch a guy or watch yourself?"

After he studies film, he hits. If the Phillies are taking early hitting that day on the field, Utley is there. If there isn't early hitting, Utley hits inside the batting cage. He spends 15 to 20 minutes hitting off the practice tee alone.

"People don't do that anymore," Thompson said.

He's right. Kids hit off the practice tee. Young kids. Kids that play tee ball. Not $85 million All-Star second basemen. After all, isn't hitting off the practice tee...

"For the birds?" Utley said. "You're moving the tee around, hitting the ball all over the place, and refining your swing to try to keep it consistent."

So it has a purpose. Everything Utley does before a game has a purpose. That's why he's so religious about his routine. And that is why he is so good.

Third Base
Mike Schmidt
1972–89

We have a consensus. Mike Schmidt is the greatest third baseman in Phillies history.

That's obvious because Schmidt is considered arguably the greatest third baseman in baseball history. So let's forget where he ranks in Phillies history in every offensive category, because we know he's at the top. Let's instead look at where he ranks among all third basemen. And remember, we're only counting his production as a third baseman. He played 157 games at first base, 24 games at shortstop, and six games at second base in his career.

Despite playing more than a full season at other positions, Schmidt ranks first in home runs (509), RBIs (1,474), and extra-base hits (940); second in slugging percentage (.526), on-base-plus-slugging percentage (.906), walks (1,411), and RCAA (582); third in RCAP (542); fourth in runs (1,418); eighth in doubles (377); ninth in on-base percentage (.380); and 12th in hits (2,059). Schmidt and Eddie Matthews are the only third basemen to hit 500 or more home runs. Schmidt is the only third basemen to have more than 1,500 RBIs. He won a National League–record 10 Gold Gloves at third base, winning nine in a row from 1976 to 1984.

"He was the best player I've ever played with," Pete Rose said. "When I say that, I'm not putting down Tony Perez. I'm not putting down Joe Morgan. I'm not putting down Johnny Bench. I'm not putting down Tom Seaver or Steve Carlton. Those are all Hall of Famers that I've played with. But Mike had the overall ability. Now, am I going to say he's better than Willie Mays or Hank Aaron or Roberto Clemente or Stan Musial? No, I'm not going to say he's better than those guys."

Rose paused.

"But he's right in the same category as those guys."

Schmidt enjoyed plenty of great moments when he played with Rose from 1979 to 1983, including being National League MVP in 1980 and 1981 and winning the World Series in 1980. But one game sticks out in Rose's mind more than any other, a game against the Montreal Expos on May 28, 1983, at Veterans Stadium.

The Phillies had been in a horrific offensive slump, and so had Schmidt. Three days earlier the Phillies had snapped a 42-inning scoreless streak, their longest offensive drought since 1942. That stretch included three consecutive shutouts. Schmidt had fared no better. He entered the May 28 game against the Expos in a 0-for-18 slump with seven strikeouts. He hadn't knocked in a run since May 4. He hadn't homered since May 3. The slump continued.

He struck out in the first inning on three pitches.

He struck out in the third on three pitches.

He struck out in the fifth on three pitches.

He struck out in the seventh on three pitches.

Twelve pitches, four strikeouts, and six runners left on base.

"That was very unusual for him, because he had such a good eye," Rose said. "People were booing him."

Schmidt dragged his carcass into the batter's box in the bottom of the ninth inning with two outs and Bob Dernier on second base in a 3–3 tie. Schmidt was buried mentally, now stuck in an 0-for-22 slump with 11 strikeouts. But Phillies fans, perhaps sensing Schmidt had hit rock bottom, stood on their feet and cheered. He kindly responded by crushing the first pitch from Jeff Reardon over the left-field wall for a two-run home run to win the game 5–3.

"So here's a guy who saw 13 pitches, 12 strikes, four strikeouts, circling the bases and he went right to Richie Ashburn to do the star of the game," Rose said.

Schmidt had little to say after the game.

"I was totally lost mentally as a hitter," he said. "I went up there just trying to stay with a fastball down and away and swinging down on the ball. I would have swung at a pitch in any location. I hit a home run, and I'm happy about that. That's it. I'm not going to talk about being 0-for-whatever or striking out. Maybe in a couple of days I will, but not now. It's been really difficult for me, because it's the first time in a while that I have heard boos on the field. So to hear the people cheering for me like that when I was basically at rock bottom is something I appreciate very, very much."

Schmidt had a love-hate relationship with Phillies fans when he played, particularly early in his career. He got booed for being too cool. He got booed for not being clutch. He got booed for striking out too much. He got booed for ripping the fans.

"Only in Philadelphia can you experience the thrill of victory one night and the agony of reading about it the next day," he said.

But it's hard to find a Phillies fan that grew up in the '70s and '80s who doesn't consider Schmidt their childhood hero. He had an incredible impact on people. The Phillies have had other talented third basemen. Dick Allen was one of the best. Scott Rolen was, too. There were others like Puddin' Head Jones, Pinky Whitney, and Dave Hollins.

But Schmidt was the best of the best. He hit .196 with 136 strikeouts in 367 at-bats in 1973, but instead of returning him to the minor leagues, the Phillies stuck with him. Their faith paid off. Schmidt hit .282 with a league-leading 36 home runs and 116 RBIs in 1974. He was on his way. He won the NL MVP three times. He made the All-Star team 12 times. He led the league in homers eight times and RBIs four times. He had a 14-year stretch from 1974 to 1987 that was unbelievable. His 511 homers in that span were 128 more than Dave Kingman, who ranked second. His 1,450 RBIs were 99 more than Jim Rice. His 937 extra-base hits were 148 more than George Brett. His 1,390 runs were 181 more than Dave Winfield.

He arguably was the best player in baseball during those 14 years.

He unarguably is the greatest player in Phillies history.

Shortstop
Jimmy Rollins
2000–Present

It is spring training 2006 and Larry Bowa is in a New York Yankees uniform at Legends Field in Tampa.

Bowa played shortstop for the Phillies for 12 seasons, from 1970 to 1981, and is one of the most popular players in franchise history. He fielded his position as well as anybody. His 1,798 hits with the Phillies are fifth in franchise history behind Mike Schmidt (2,234), Richie Ashburn (2,217), Ed Delahanty (2,213), and Del Ennis (1,812). He made five All-Star Games with the Phillies (1974, 1975, 1976, 1978, and 1979) and finished third in National League MVP voting in 1978. But as Bowa began his first season as the New York Yankees' third-base coach, Jimmy Rollins began his seventh season with the Phillies. Bowa and Rollins had an interesting relationship while Bowa managed the Phillies from 2001 to 2004. Bowa could talk. Rollins could talk. Rollins once purchased a new wardrobe for Bowa because he thought his was outdated. One day as Bowa walked through the Phillies clubhouse at Citizens Bank Park, Rollins told Bowa that he should drag his back foot a little more when he walked.

"Pimp that walk," Rollins said.

"Why don't you drag that back foot across home plate every once in a while?" Bowa chirped back.

Rollins laughed.

But on this March afternoon in Tampa, Bowa was asked if Rollins could be considered a better shortstop than himself—the five-time All-Star, MVP candidate, and World Series champion.

"Nah, I need to see Jimmy play a little bit longer before I say that," Bowa said.

Fair enough. Rollins hit .277 with 25 homers and 83 RBIs in 2006. He won the NL MVP in 2007, when he hit .296 with 38 doubles, 20 triples, 30 home runs, 94 RBIs, 41 stolen bases, and 139 runs scored. He was the first National League shortstop to be MVP since Barry Larkin in 1996 and just the second since Maury Wills in 1962.

Fast-forward to Dodger Stadium in 2008. Bowa is the third-base coach for the Los Angeles Dodgers and is asked if he is ready to call Rollins the better Phillies shortstop. Bowa didn't hesitate.

"I wasn't a great player. I was a good player," Bowa said. "Jimmy is a great player. Yeah, I think he's a great player. He knows what he's doing. Just talking with him, it seems like he's mentally where you're supposed to be at. I think when he first came up he was like anybody else. He sort of fought the system a little bit. Then you go through your trials and tribulations and you learn from the things you do. But he's well grounded now and he's got the chance to be up there with the all-time people that have played that position."

That's a pretty bold statement. Could Rollins really finish his career among shortstops like Ernie Banks, Cal Ripken Jr., Derek Jeter, and Ozzie Smith?

"I think so," Bowa said. "He does everything. He's got great hands. He's got a great arm. He's got great instincts running the bases. Sometimes hitting the 30 home runs might not have been a good deal, sometimes you get carried away with that. But he's capable of hitting them 15 to 20 easy. Jimmy is the total package."

Rollins finished the 2009 season ranked first in doubles (350), triples (95), home runs (145), RBIs (620), runs (945), stolen bases (292), extra-base hits (590), on-base-plus-slugging percentage (.768), and slugging percentage (.439). He ranked second in average (.275) and hits (1,627) and seventh in on-base percentage (.329). He finished the season with a .983 fielding percentage, the second-best percentage in baseball history. Only Omar Vizquel (.985) is better. Bowa ranked fifth at .980.

"He's as good as anybody in the league," Bowa said. "And I know there are some good ones. Hanley Ramirez is a good one in Florida. Miguel Tejada is very good both ways. There are some good shortstops, but he's right up there with all of them."

Time will tell how good Rollins eventually is, but *The Bill James Handbook 2010* thinks Rollins has a chance to put up some phenomenal numbers before he leaves the game. It gave him a 25 percent chance to get 3,000 hits and a 4 percent chance to break Tris Speaker's record of 792 doubles. Obviously, some of those milestones are long shots, but the fact that he even has a chance says something about his ability.

Should Rollins stay healthy and productive, he has a real chance to get 3,000 hits. He does that, and we're talking Hall of Fame. Only 27 players in baseball history have 3,000 or more hits. Of those, only Pete Rose, Craig Biggio, and Rafael Palmeiro aren't in the Hall of Fame. It's only a matter of time before Biggio is there. Rose and Palmeiro are a different story because of gambling and steroids.

Does Rollins have more seasons like 2007 in him? His numbers dipped in 2008 and 2009, but he said he doesn't consider 2007 a career year. He said he thinks he can have many more years like that in the future.

"I plan on it," Rollins said.

Even if he doesn't, compare Rollins to Bowa and other top shortstops in Phillies history, like Dave Bancroft (1915–20) and

Granny Hamner (1944–59), and it's no contest. Should Rollins never play another game for the Phillies, he is the greatest shortstop in Phillies history. And by the time he is finished, he could be considered one of the best of all time.

Left Field
Greg Luzinski
1970–80

Talk to baseball historians, and they probably would say Ed Delahanty is the greatest hitter in Phillies history.

They might be right. His plaque in the National Baseball Hall of Fame and Museum reads, "One of the game's greatest sluggers." Sam Crawford, the Hall of Fame right fielder for the Cincinnati Reds (1899–1902) and Detroit Tigers (1903–17), once said, "I think Ed was the best right-handed hitter I ever saw." The *Cleveland Plain-Dealer* in 1936 asked Bill Dinneen, a four-time 20-game winner in a career that lasted from 1898 to 1909, about New York Yankees rookie Joe DiMaggio, and Dinneen compared him to Delahanty.

"This is the closest replica to Del I have ever seen," he said. "The bat he uses, the way he swings, the manner in which he watches balls he doesn't offer at, are reminiscent of Del. In the outfield, DiMag simply emphasizes the likeness of the old-time star, the way he catches balls, runs, and throws. His every move is taken from the same baseball mold that cast Ed Delahanty."

Delahanty, who played for the Phillies from 1888 to 1889 and 1891 to 1901, hit .348 in his Phillies career. His .346 career average ranks fifth in baseball history. Only Ty Cobb (.366), Rogers Hornsby (.359), Joe Jackson (.356), and Lefty O'Doul (.349) were better. But it's simply impossible to compare baseball in the 19th century to baseball in the 20th century. Sure, they played nine innings. Sure, they had bats and balls and ran around a diamond. But those are about the only things that resemble the modern game from the game in its infancy.

So we're not considering Delahanty or Sherry Magee (1904–14) as the greatest left fielder in Phillies history. Historians might think we're nuts, but we think we have found a pretty solid alternative in Greg "the Bull" Luzinski. He gets a spot on this team over left fielders Del Ennis and Pat Burrell.

Luzinski enjoyed a six-season stretch from 1973 to 1978 when he was one of the best hitters in baseball. In fact, he ranked sixth in home runs (165) and third in RBIs (591) in that span. Mike Schmidt (189), Reggie Jackson (183), Bobby Bonds (170), Dave Kingman (169), and Jeff Burroughs (166) were the only players to hit more homers than Luzinski from '73 to '78. Jackson (612) and Johnny Bench (599) were the only players to have more RBIs. Luzinski finished in the top 10 in the National League MVP race each year from 1975 to 1978, establishing himself as one of the most feared hitters of the 1970s. He finished second in MVP voting to Joe Morgan in 1975, when he hit .300 with 34 home runs and 120 RBIs. He finished second in MVP voting to George Foster in 1977, when he hit .309 with 39 homers and 130 RBIs.

Luzinski had heard then that Morgan, who received 21 of the 23 first-place votes, won in '75 because the Cincinnati Reds won the National League West, while the Phillies had finished second behind the Pittsburgh Pirates in the NL East. But in '77, when the Phillies won a National League–best 101 games to win the East, he finished second behind Foster, who hit 52 home runs, despite the fact the Reds finished second in the West. The voting in '77 was much closer than in '75, when Luzinski received no first-place votes and finished with 154 points to Morgan's 321. Foster received 15 first-place votes in '77 and finished with 291 points compared to Luzinski, who received nine first-place votes and finished with 255.

"I felt like I had a pretty good chance in '77," Luzinski said. "Believe it or not, I'm kind of at the point where I think back and I just say to myself, 'I wasn't supposed to win them.' I don't know. It's just a feeling I have. I wasn't supposed to win them. I was a big guy at that time. People used to criticize me because I was too heavy, this and that. But I put some numbers on the board for those four years, especially that one year."

He could have put up even better numbers in that four-year run, except he hit behind Schmidt in three of those seasons.

BULL AND BOWA

Larry Bowa and Greg Luzinski became close friends early in their professional baseball careers, but it wasn't love at first sight.

During instructional league one year, Luzinski was playing first base and Bowa was playing shortstop. There was a double-play ball, but the runner slid so hard into second base that Bowa didn't throw to first.

"Don't be afraid of a little contact," Luzinski hollered to Bowa.

The inning ended and Bowa entered the dugout. He couldn't make out what Luzinski had said on the field.

"What did you say?" Bowa said.

"I said, 'Don't be afraid of a little contact,'" Luzinski said.

Bowa, in Luzinski's words, "got pissed off." And to make matters worse, Luzinski later learned he had to be roommates with Bowa.

"He was in my ear the entire way back on the bus, and I took it because I figured he's a little guy and I just met him," Luzinski said. "Now I've got to room with him. I'm moving my bags and he starts up on me again. I said, 'Bo, I've had enough.' About that time I went across the bed, I grabbed him by the shirt, pulled him to me, and as I went to hit him…"

Crack!

But Luzinski didn't punch Bowa. He punched teammate John Vukovich square in the jaw instead. Vukovich, who grew up with Bowa in Sacramento, had stepped in to break up the fight between the bigger Luzinski and the smaller Bowa. Vukovich took Luzinski's punch and flew against the wall.

Boom!

Manager Bob Wellman, who was staying in the room next to Luzinski and Bowa, immediately knocked on their door.

"Everything all right in there?" he said.

"There's no problem," Luzinski said.

"No, no, no, no," Bowa said. "There's no problem."

"Yeah, there is," Vukovich said. "I've got a sore jaw."

Luzinski laughed as he recalled the story.

"That was the only time that I ever went after Bo," he said. "And after that we became best of friends. But poor Vuke got hit in the jaw."

Bowa could get under Luzinski's skin like few could, but Bowa said he learned when Bull had reached his boiling point.

"A couple times I went a little too far. He'd give me that look," Bowa said. "But I always knew I could outrun him."

"I would have had a few more RBIs," Luzinski said with a laugh. "He picked a few up, obviously."

Bull didn't mind.

"Even though it's an individual game, that's part of the team," he said. "That's all part of the batting order and part of the team, trying to protect the guy in front of you so they pitch to him. That's the reason you're in those spots. We had great teams. We were on last-place teams in the early '70s and graduated to those Eastern Division–winning ballclubs and finally winning it in 1980. I saw both sides of it. I'd rather be on the other side when you can say you're a world champion because obviously there are lots of guys that don't get there."

Remove Delahanty and Magee from the equation, and Luzinski ranks first among left fielders in Phillies history in doubles (245), extra-base hits (486), slugging percentage (.490), RCAA (219), and RCAP (132); second in average (.280), hits (1,267), home runs (220), on-base percentage (.363), on-base-plus-slugging percentage (.853), RBIs (796), runs (605), and walks (557).

Imagine what numbers Luzinski could have put up if he had played today.

"It's an offensive game now, no question about it," he said. "You look at the ballparks. You look at the bats. Baseballs obviously are different. We had two bat companies back then. Now there's 15 to 20. Players are bigger, stronger, that type of thing. Obviously, there were fewer teams then, so less positions to be filled on big-league rosters. So, I mean, obviously people look back at some point and say our era was a pretty good era compared to the era today. There's no pitching, blah, blah, blah. I can remember packing the bat bag, going to New York and facing [Tom] Seaver and [Jerry] Koosman. Or in Houston with J.R. Richard, Nolan Ryan, and Larry Dierker. That's three quality starters right there. There were quality pitchers. We saw their best and went from there."

And Bull hit them all. Could Delahanty have hit them? He was one of the most feared hitters in his era, so if he played in the '70s you'd have to think he would have. But we will never know. Let's call Delahanty the greatest player in Phillies history before 1900, but let's call Luzinski the greatest left fielder in Phillies history in the modern era.

Center Field
Richie Ashburn
1948–59

Don Richard Ashburn had his share of nicknames.

Richie. Putt Putt. Whitey. His Whiteness. But some of the top National League outfielders in the 1950s and early 1960s had a different nickname for Ashburn, who beats Lenny Dykstra, Billy Hamilton, Roy Thomas, Cy Williams, Garry Maddox, and others as the best center fielder in Phillies history.

"We called him Little Boy," Willie Mays said.

Ashburn, inducted into the Hall of Fame in 1995, made the NL All-Star team five times in his 15-year career, 12 of which he spent with the Phillies. He started in center field in the 1948 and 1951 All-Star Games but made the team as a reserve in 1953, 1958, and 1962. It was tough to break the starting lineup back then with Mays, Hank Aaron, Roberto Clemente, and others in the outfield. So Mays kidded Ashburn about it.

"We always would point at him and say, 'There goes the Little Boy. He can't do anything,'" Mays said good-naturedly. "But he was hitting .340. We'd hit .319, but Richie would hit .340. But he couldn't get in there. Where was he going to play? We would always tell him that, 'You can't play with us. You've got to go

Willie Mays (left), center fielder for the San Francisco Giants, and Richie Ashburn, center fielder for the Philadelphia Phillies, talk while kneeling on the field, circa 1955.

home. You can't play.' That's what we did in the All-Star Game. We had a lot of fun. Nobody was jealous of anybody. We just had fun. We'd talk to each other. And whatever we had to do to win, that's what we did. And Richie was right in the crowd there. He was a nice man. He had such a good humor that we always loved him."

Ashburn hit .308 with 29 home runs and 586 RBIs in his career. Those numbers don't pop when compared to outfielders like Mays, Aaron, and Clemente, but Ashburn wasn't a power hitter. He was a runner and a hitter. He had more hits in the '50s than anybody in the majors with 1,875. That's more hits than Nellie Fox (1,837), Stan Musial (1,771), Al Dark (1,675), and Duke Snider (1,605). Ashburn scored 952 runs in the '50s. Only Mickey Mantle (994) and Snider (970) scored more. Ashburn also led the league in on-base percentage, hits, and walks three times while he played with the Phillies from 1948 to 1959.

"Richard, as a hitter, he would bunt for a base hit and then he would go for hits," Mays said. "He may hit five home runs a year, but he could run."

Ashburn, who never hit more than four homers in a season with the Phillies, won two batting titles, the first in 1955 and the second in 1958. He hit .338 in 1955 to win comfortably over Mays, who finished second at .319. Mays finished second to Ashburn again in '58, and that time it was much closer. Ashburn was hitting .338 after the first game of a doubleheader against the Pittsburgh Pirates on September 22. Mays was hitting .342. But Ashburn hit .667 (14-for-21) in his final five games to finish at .350, while Mays hit .476 (10-for-21) to finish at .347. Talk about a remarkable final week. If Mays got two hits, Ashburn got three. If Mays got three hits, Ashburn got four.

Both players set career highs in batting average that year.

"I only hit 29 home runs that year," Mays said. "I should have hit more, but I was trying to win the battling championship to show people I could do everything. Richard must have looked in the paper and saw me pretty close. A guy called me the next day after the season ended and said, 'Guess what, Willie?' I said, 'What's going on?' He said, 'Richard bunted four times to beat you.' I called him up and said, 'Hey, man, what's wrong with you? Swing the bat. It's late in the season. Nobody is worried about the bunt.'"

Mays laughed.

"He was a really nice man," he said. "He was fun to play against."

Offensively, Ashburn was a fantastic leadoff man. He could hit. He could walk. He could run. He fattened the production numbers for players like Del Ennis, Puddin' Head Jones, and others. But he saved as many runs as he scored. Ashburn is one of the best defensive outfielders of all time.

Few, if any, in baseball history covered as much ground as Ashburn. Ashburn (also known as Putt Putt, a nickname Ted Williams gave him because he said Ashburn ran like he had twin motors in his pants) ranks sixth in baseball history with 6,089 putouts in the outfield. Only Mays (7,095), Tris Speaker (6,792), Rickey Henderson (6,466), Max Carey (6,363), and Ty Cobb (6,360) had more. But it's worth noting that Ashburn's career lasted 15 seasons. Henderson (25 seasons), Cobb (24 seasons) Mays (22 seasons), Speaker (22 seasons), and Carey (20 seasons) had much longer careers to add to their totals. Ashburn could have played longer, but he retired after the 1962 season with the New York Mets, despite the fact that he hit .306, because he said he couldn't stand the losing.

In his 12-year career with the Phillies, which ran from 1948 through 1959, Ashburn had an incredible 5,454 putouts. The next closest in that span? Larry Doby, who had 3,616. To put Ashburn's 12-year putout total in comparison, Mays had 4,784 putouts from 1954 to 1965, his first uninterrupted 12-year run in the majors.

"He could field," Mays said. "His arm wasn't real strong, but he could field. He got a good jump on the ball. Oh yeah."

Ashburn's ability to hit, run, and catch the baseball is why he finishes at the top over other Phillies center fielders like Dykstra, who had the best individual season of any Phillies center fielder in 1993. Ashburn also helped the Whiz Kids win the National League pennant in 1950. There's something to be said for that, too. Philadelphia loves a winner, and Ashburn was one.

Right Field
Bobby Abreu
1998–2006

It was mentioned to a highly regarded baseball man that Bobby Abreu could be the best right fielder in Phillies history.

"Abreu?" he said disdainfully.

Yes, Abreu. Better than Chuck Klein. Better than Johnny Callison.

"Callison? Abreu? Don't even say their names in the same sentence," he said. "Abreu put up stats."

He did. He put up remarkable numbers. He leads Phillies right fielders in extra-base hits (585), doubles (348), stolen bases (254), and walks (947). He is second in hits (1,474), home runs (195), runs (891), on-base percentage (.416), slugging percentage (.513), and on-base-plus-slugging percentage (.928). He is third in RBIs (814). He is fourth in hitting (.303) among right fielders with 2,000 or more plate appearances.

"He's so patient and he has such good bat control," Charlie Manuel said. "He takes the ball to all fields. When he's going good, he doesn't try to overdo it. He's one of the most confident hitters I've ever seen."

Abreu was derided in Philadelphia because he wouldn't sacrifice his body to make a catch against the right-field fence and occasionally looked indifferent to his job. Fans said he didn't hit well when it mattered most. Of course, his inability to hit in the clutch wasn't true. In his eight full seasons with the Phillies (1998–2005) he hit better with runners in scoring position than his overall season average six times and better in close and late situations, which are plate appearances in the seventh inning or later with the batting team tied, ahead by one, or the tying run at least on deck, four times. Abreu might not have crashed into the wall, but he did everything else very well.

But how can Abreu be better than Klein, who is in the Hall of Fame?

Klein might be one of the most overrated players in baseball history. He put up superhuman numbers from 1929 to 1933, arguably the best five years ever to start a big-league career. Klein led the majors in hits (1,118), doubles (232), and extra-base hits (458) in that five-year span. He finished second in runs (658). He finished fourth in home runs (180), slugging percentage (.636), and OPS (1.050). He finished fifth in RBIs (693) and eighth in OBP (.414). He won the Triple Crown in 1933. But the left-handed-hitting Klein also played at Baker Bowl. Baker Bowl had a right-field fence that stood just 280½ feet down the line from home plate. To put that into perspective, at Lamade Stadium, the

Bobby Abreu bats during the game against the Boston Red Sox at Citizens Bank Park on May 21, 2006. The Phillies defeated the Red Sox 10–5.

ballpark where the Little League hosts its World Series every summer in Williamsport, Pennsylvania, its fence sits 225 feet from home plate.

In other words, Klein had to hit the ball just 55½ feet farther than a 12-year-old Little Leaguer for a home run.

Sure, the Baker Bowl had a 40-foot-high fence that eventually increased to 60 feet. But pop flies that would have been outs elsewhere were home runs, and any sort of line drive meant an automatic hit. Hitters loved playing at Baker Bowl. Pitchers loathed it.

"It was an easy target," said Lefty O'Doul, who played for the Phillies from 1929 to 1930. "Every time I went to bat, I looked at that high fence and I felt sure I could hit it. That old fence sure gave me some confidence."

"Everybody aimed for right," Dick Bartell, the National League's first all-star shortstop, said in his book *Rowdy Richard*. "I've seen high fly balls the second baseman could go out and catch come down against the fence for doubles."

Klein clearly benefited from this, just like every left-handed hitter did. He hit .391 at home and .321 on the road in 1929, .439 at home and .332 on the road in 1930, .407 at home and .266 on the road in 1931, and .423 at home and .266 on the road in 1932. Klein's Triple Crown season? He hit .467 at Baker Bowl and just .280 on the road.

The Elias Sports Bureau found that from 1928 through 1933, Klein hit .420 with 131 homers and 468 RBIs in 411 games at home and .296 with 60 homers and 258 RBIs in 412 games on the road. Those are some severely lopsided splits that only reinforce the fact that Klein isn't the best right fielder in Phillies history, Hall of Fame plaque in Cooperstown, N.Y., or not. In fact, if he hadn't played at Baker Bowl the first five-plus seasons of his career, few would remember him today. He certainly wouldn't be in the Hall of Fame.

Callison? He remains a popular choice and certainly is worthy of consideration, but his numbers simply don't compare to Abreu's. Callison probably would have been the National League

NO KLEIN? SERIOUSLY?

Can this team really not have Chuck Klein in its lineup?

Guess we just couldn't get over his splits at Baker Bowl vs. on the road. We just couldn't get over the fact that his peak lasted just five years in a bandbox. But because Klein is in the Hall of Fame, we thought we'd ask the National Baseball Hall of Fame and Museum for a little perspective.

"His five years were so great," Hall of Fame researcher Gabriel Schechter said. "Sandy Koufax only had five great years. Dizzy Dean only had a few great years. There are a lot of Hall of Famers who had just a handful of great years. Klein's great years were fantastic. And, yes, there is the home-away differential. And when he came back to the Phillies, he started hitting again. But my viewpoint is nobody else on the team or in the league was hitting the way he was. He won a Triple Crown. That's got to carry some weight."

From 1928 to 1933, Klein hit .420 at Baker Bowl vs .296 on the road. That is a 124-point differential.

"He was just fine on the road and amazing at home," Schechter said. "Look at a guy like Todd Helton. It'll be interesting when these Colorado players come up on the ballot. Larry Walker, Andres Galarraga, Todd Helton. People will look at the home-road differentials and say these guys were phenomenal in Colorado but very good on the road, too."

Interestingly, Helton's home-road differential (.068 points) and Walker's home-road differential (.070 points) are a little less than half the difference of Klein's, although Schechter makes a valid point in that Klein shouldn't be penalized for playing in a hitter's park.

"I don't think it's a case of taking a mediocre player and having his stats inflated," he said. "He was a very good player and took advantage of his own ballpark. You still have to hit the ball."

But a home-road differential almost twice as large as Helton and Walker, who played at hitter-friendly Coors Field, only proves how much of an advantage Klein had and how he wouldn't have been close to the same player elsewhere.

MVP in 1964 had the Phillies not choked in the final weeks of the season to lose the pennant. He earned MVP honors in the '64 All-Star Game after he hit a two-out, three-run home run in the bottom of the ninth inning off Dick Radatz to beat the American League 7–4 at Shea Stadium. But Callison's run of greatness had a short four-year window from 1962 to 1965. He had 23, 26, 31, and 32 homers in those four seasons, respectively. He also had 83, 78, 104, and 101 RBIs, respectively. He never had more than 16 homers or 64 RBIs in any other season with the Phillies. Callison certainly was a far superior outfielder than Abreu. He had a remarkable arm that few tested. But his defensive prowess can't outweigh Abreu's offensive prowess and the longevity of his career.

"He had a great bat," the baseball lifer said in Callison's defense. "If you take all the athletes that played baseball, and all the best athletes played baseball then, and you condense them down, a lot of organizations had 300 minor-league players in their system. So the crop you were picking from was a whole different aspect than what the game is now. You weren't going to miss Don Drysdale or Sandy Koufax or Johnny Podres. They pitched every fourth day."

Callison had a .795 OPS in his Phillies career, which was .025 points better than other right fielders in that span. Abreu had a .933 OPS with the Phillies from 1998 to 2005, which was .104 points better than other right fielders in that span. In other words, putting nostalgia aside, Abreu was a better right fielder in his era with the Phillies than Callison was in his era with the Phillies. And while Abreu never seemed to play with much emotion, he produced.

THE DREAM TEAM: THE PITCHERS

THE ROTATION
Steve Carlton
1972–86

There have been thousands of left-handed pitchers in baseball, but only three known as "Lefty" have plaques in the Hall of Fame:

Lefty Gomez.

Lefty Grove.

Steve Carlton.

Carlton, known as Lefty to his peers, finished his remarkable career with 329 victories. No other left-handed pitcher has won more games except Warren Spahn, who won 363. Carlton ranks 11th in baseball history in victories. He ranks fourth in strikeouts with 4,136. He won four Cy Young Awards with the Phillies. He finished in the top 10 in National League MVP voting five times with the Phillies. He made 10 NL All-Star teams, seven with the Phillies.

"When he pitched we used to call it Win Day," said former teammate Gary Matthews, who played with Carlton from 1981 to 1983.

Carlton pitched for the Phillies from 1972 to 1986, but look at an 11-year stretch from '72 to '82, the seasons in which he won his four Cy Young Awards. He led the National League in wins (208), strikeouts (2,483), and complete games (176). He tied Don Sutton and Tom Seaver with 32 shutouts. He finished second in

Pitcher Steve Carlton during a mid-1970s game at Veterans Stadium in Philadelphia. Carlton played for the Phillies from 1972 to 1986.

innings pitched (3,009⅔ innings) behind Phil Niekro (3,031⅓ innings). He had a 2.96 ERA, which ranked third behind Seaver (2.87 ERA) and Sutton (2.91 ERA).

Carlton, who joined the Phillies in a February 25, 1972, trade with the St. Louis Cardinals for Rick Wise, went 27–10 with a 1.97 ERA in his first season with the Phillies, a terrible team that finished 59–97. Carlton won a record 45.8 percent of his team's games that year. He was just the fifth pitcher in history to win 20 games for a last-place team. He won 15 straight decisions in 1972. He threw eight shutouts. He completed 30 games. Nobody other than Catfish Hunter has thrown 30 complete games since Carlton in 1972. Hunter threw 30 in 1975.

Carlton went 13–20 in '73, 16–13 in '74, and 15–14 in '75. He went 20–7 in '76, but the eccentric Carlton found his mojo after the Phillies hired Eagles trainer Gus Hoefling in 1977. Hoefling had a kung fu background, and Carlton took to Hoefling's practices immediately. His practices included garbage cans filled with rice that Carlton could sink into to build muscles by moving his arms, wrists, or legs. Carlton went 23–10 with a 2.64 ERA in '77 to win his second Cy Young.

"He was ahead of his time," said Tim McCarver, Carlton's personal catcher with the Phillies. "He was ahead of his time with visualization. I used to think he was in napping, but he was visualizing. He told me a lot later, much later after he retired, that the more he thought about the outside and inside lanes of the plate, the more he would stay away from the middle. And because of that, he did. He was reading really heavy stuff back in those days, and nobody really could keep up with him. There were the buckets of rice and stuff like that. Steve really believed in Gus, and Gus was the perfect guy for Lefty. All that stuff about the training regimen was absolutely true. Oh yeah."

But it wasn't buckets of rice that made Carlton a Hall of Fame pitcher. He had incredible talent.

He also had that slider. Hitting it was like "trying to drink coffee with a fork," Willie Stargell said.

"The one thing that I did was I called for his slider more," McCarver said. "Just go with his strength and for the most part you'll go through them like tissue paper. I was there in St. Louis with the genesis of that pitch back in 1969. It was [Bob] Gibson on the trip to Japan where he talked to Steve about the grip of the slider. And Steve said, 'Well, if I make my arm strong...' He was the strongest from his fingertips to his elbow of any man I've ever met. Therefore he didn't have to rotate the elbow. He just cut through the ball. And that cut through the ball not only made the slider devastating, but it protected his arm at the same time. He never really had elbow problems. He had shoulder problems but never elbow problems."

Davey Lopes hit .382 in his career against Carlton. The only hitter to have 50 or more plate appearances against Carlton and hit him better was Jesus Alou, who hit an unbelievable .436 against him. But despite his success against Lefty, Lopes always respected Carlton's slider. In fact, anybody who mentions Carlton almost immediately mentions it.

"It came down and in," Lopes said. "Everybody used to talk about [Ron] Guidry's slider, but the difference between Guidry's slider and Steve's slider is that Guidry threw his slider out of the strike zone. Guys chased it a lot, down and in. Steve's slider hit the corners and that kind of stuff. He back-doored you. He threw it on the inside corner. That was a little different. You hear about quality sliders, but he had as good a slider for a left-hander that I have ever seen."

Carlton went 24–9 with a 2.34 ERA to pick up his third Cy Young in 1980, when the Phillies won their first World Series. He went 23–11 with a 3.10 ERA in 1982, when he won his fourth Cy Young.

"It's easier to get up for pitchers like that," Matthews said. "It's easier to get up when Cole Hamels or Lefty is pitching. They're going to be right there. They're going to keep you in the game. You should feel that way with other guys, but when they're standing up there, ball one, ball four, and never around the dish, it's hard to get ready for that."

Teammates were always ready for Lefty.

How couldn't you be ready for Win Day?

Robin Roberts
1948–61

The best pitcher in baseball in the 1950s was...

Warren Spahn? Whitey Ford? Early Wynn? Don Newcombe? How about Robin Roberts?

"He was the top pitcher at that time," Willie Mays said.

"It's a compliment," Roberts said. "I certainly enjoyed it. I just showed up and pitched."

Roberts dominated the '50s. He won 199 games, more than anybody except Spahn, who won 202. Roberts, inducted into the Hall of Fame in 1976, won 20 or more games each season from 1950 through 1955. He won 19 games in 1956. He led the National League in strikeouts (1,516), complete games (237), and innings pitched (3,012) in the '50s. He finished second behind Spahn with 30 shutouts. He finished fourth behind Spahn, Johnny Altonelli, and Sal Maglie with a 3.32 ERA. He threw an astounding 28 straight complete games from 1952 to 1953. He also started for the National League in the 1950, 1951, 1953, 1954, and 1955 All-Star Games.

"First of all, he had control," Mays said. "He didn't have a good curveball. He had a good fastball that he controlled in and out. He'd never knock you down, but he was quick. He knew what he was doing. I could hit him pretty good, but I never hit home runs against him. I think I hit one home run off him in the last game of a series in '56. I just scraped the scoreboard in the Polo Grounds. He threw a curveball to me. He never did throw that curveball to me again."

But Mays had his hands full without the breaking ball.

"He was a hard pitcher," he said.

The Cy Young didn't come into existence until 1956, but Roberts finished in the top 10 in National League MVP voting five times in the 1950s. He won The Sporting News' Pitcher of the Year Award in 1952 and 1955. He went 28–7 with a 2.59 ERA in 1952, his best season in the majors. No National League pitcher had won 28 games since 1935, when Dizzy Dean won 28 for the St. Louis Cardinals. No National League pitcher has won that many games since.

Roberts led the league in wins four times (1952–55), innings five times (1951–55), strikeouts twice (1953–54), and complete games five times (1952–56). And despite all those innings, he never walked more than 77 batters in a season.

"He had real good control," said catcher Stan Lopata, who was Roberts' teammate from 1948 to 1958. "He had a good fastball. He had a little movement on it. We've seen pitchers with better breaking balls, but his big asset was his control. He made them hit. He figured, *Hey, I have eight guys out there. Let them earn their money.* He had such an easy motion. It snuck up on you. You'd think, *Hey, man, I can hit this guy.* And then the ball is by you. That easy motion fooled a lot of guys. Yep, they'd all say they could hit him, but they never did."

That was why Roberts rarely worried about base-runners.

"There weren't too many ballclubs that would steal in the National League, but Andy Seminick and myself would say, 'Hey, Robbie, how about giving us a chance and hold these guys on?'" Lopata said. "He would say, 'If they steal second base and third base, they've still got to score from third. Don't worry about it.' That's the attitude he had. And he got them out, too. That's the confidence he had."

In his only postseason in 1950, Roberts started Game 2 of the World Series against the New York Yankees at Shibe Park. He allowed 10 hits, two runs, three walks, and struck out five in 10 innings in a 2–1 loss. He allowed a solo home run to Joe DiMaggio in the tenth inning to lose the game. Roberts pitched a scoreless inning in relief in Game 4 to finish the Series 0–1 with a 1.64 ERA.

"I was on a good club," Roberts said. "We were a good team when I won 20 games. When we weren't a good team I didn't win 20 games."

But Roberts is being modest. The Phillies only had three winning seasons in the '50s, so he won on some teams that played pretty poorly. On the other hand, Spahn's Milwaukee Braves had eight winning seasons in the '50s. Put Roberts on a better team, and he probably would have won a few more games. He probably would have won at least 300. He finished 286–245 with a 3.40 ERA in a career that lasted from 1948 to 1966.

He started 609 games. He threw an astounding 305 complete games.

"I just assumed that I was going to pitch a complete game," Roberts said. "I did a lot of times. And in the ones I came out they pinch-hit for me late in the game. So a number I could have finished, but didn't."

He paused.

"But there also were a number of them I shouldn't have finished and I did," he said, laughing.

But as good as Roberts was, it is a little surprising today that he is not more recognized for his accomplishments outside of Philadelphia. There are reasons for that. The Phillies made just one World Series with Roberts. The New York Yankees went eight times. The Brooklyn Dodgers went four times (the Los Angeles Dodgers won the World Series in 1959). The Braves went twice with Spahn. Roberts often jokes that he is not the most recognized Robin Roberts today. The broadcaster is.

"A lot of my friends have gone to the television when they heard Robin Roberts was coming on," he said. "They saw a prettier picture than me, I'll tell you that."

But she couldn't pitch like Roberts.

"Oh, people know about Robin Roberts," Mays said. "You may not hear it too much, but they know about him. Even if the fans don't know, the players do, because he was one of the special pitchers."

Grover Cleveland Alexander
1911–17, 1930

Grover Cleveland Alexander battled his personal demons as often as he battled Rogers Hornsby and Honus Wagner.

He fared better against Hornsby and Wagner.

Alexander won 373 games in his 20-year career, eight of which he spent with the Phillies. Only Cy Young (511) and Walter Johnson (417) have won more games. He is third in Phillies history with 190 wins. His 2.18 ERA is the best for any Phillies pitcher with 1,000 or more innings. He leads the franchise with 61 shutouts. He is second in complete games with 220. He is fifth in strikeouts with 1,409. He won 30 or more games from 1915 to 1917 before the Phillies traded him to the Cubs.

But while Alexander, inducted into the Hall of Fame in 1938, regularly won on the mound, he lost his battle with alcoholism. In fact, later in life he warned people to stay away from alcohol. Alexander, who also suffered from epilepsy, even warned Robin Roberts about it. Roberts, who broke Alexander's franchise record for wins May 13, 1958, crossed paths with him long before he ever put on a Phillies uniform. Roberts grew up in Springfield, Illinois, and attended East Pleasant Hill School. Roberts' school held a sports banquet near the end of his eighth-grade year, and Alexander was the guest speaker because he happened to be staying in a hotel in town.

"He had had a tough time with drinking," Roberts said. "The hotel operator in our hometown in Springfield was John Connor. He took care of him. He let Alexander stay there."

One of Roberts' teachers knew Alexander stayed at the hotel, which was how he got him to speak.

"Boys, I must tell you, baseball is a wonderful game," Alexander said. "But don't take to drink. Look what it did to me."

That's about all he said.

"I guess he figured he had said enough," Roberts said.

But the short speech certainly made an impression on Roberts.

"It was so interesting," he said. "When I won my 191st with the Phillies, I remember thinking of that night that he was at that banquet. It was one of those things that people think you made it up."

Alexander had three unbelievable years with the Phillies from 1915 to 1917. He went 31–10 with a 1.22 ERA in 1915, when he led the Phillies to the World Series for the first time in franchise history. He started 49 games and threw 36 complete games and 12 shutouts. He went 33–12 with a 1.55 ERA in 1916, throwing 16 shutouts. He went 30–13 with a 1.83 ERA in 1917, throwing eight shutouts. He put up those numbers pitching half his games at Baker Bowl, a notorious hitter's park.

He survived Baker Bowl because he kept the ball down.

"His sinking fastball seemed fashioned from cement," Roger Kahn wrote in *The Head Game*. "No one consistently hit it into the air."

Roberts' coach with the Phillies, Cy Perkins, caught for the Philadelphia Athletics from 1915 to 1930. He knew Alexander and his pitching philosophy well.

"He said he was talking to Alexander one day and he said, 'Throw strikes. Different curves,'" Roberts said. "Evidently he was kind of a closed-mouthed guy."

Perkins later told Roberts that he considered him one of the five best pitchers he had ever seen. Walter Johnson, Lefty Grove, Herb Pennock, and Alexander were the others. Alexander and Roberts are considered the two best right-handed pitchers in Phillies history.

"I go with him," said Roberts, when asked who is better. "It's close, but I've got to go with him. He had a better curveball."

The Phillies got Alexander when Patsy O'Rourke, who scouted for Phillies owner Horace Fogel, spotted him late in the summer of 1910 while playing for Syracuse in the New York State League.

"See anything up there that caught your eye?" Fogel asked.

"You bet, Mr. Fogel," O'Rourke said. "A fine pitcher. One of the greatest pitching prospects I've ever looked at."

Fogel thought O'Rourke was talking about George Chalmers, whom the Phillies had already signed.

"Chalmers is good, but the fella I'm talking about, Alexander, is even better," O'Rourke said. "All I can say is that you better grab this Alexander before someone else does."

Fogel got Alexander for $750. It was a steal even then. Alexander went 28–13 with a 2.57 ERA in his rookie season for the Phillies in 1911. He made 37 starts, completed 31 games, and threw seven shutouts. He led the National League in wins five times with the Phillies. He won the pitching Triple Crown—most wins, most strikeouts, and lowest ERA—in 1915 and 1916. He won Game 1 of the 1915 World Series.

The Phillies traded him a little more than two years later.

Alexander famously won Games 2 and 6 of the 1926 World Series with the St. Louis Cardinals. He supposedly got drunk after Game 6 because he didn't expect to pitch in Game 7. Of course, he did, and legend has it that he was hung over when he entered the game with the bases loaded and two outs in the seventh inning to face New York Yankees slugger Tony Lazzeri.

He struck out Lazzeri on a nasty curveball.

That pitch made Alexander so famous that Ronald Reagan played him in the movie *The Winning Team*. But Alexander didn't have much success after he retired in 1930. He worked in a flea circus near Times Square. He floated from place to place and job to job, consumed by his drinking.

"I had control of everything but myself," Alexander told the *Philadelphia Evening Bulletin* in 1939. "Control of bats, but none with dollars. But that's the way I've been. I've made promises and broke them, the way I broke a curve outside to heavy hitters. I've laughed as many times as I've cried, so I guess I'm even with life."

Jim Bunning
1964–67, 1970–71

Jim Bunning could put fear into the hearts and minds of men that wouldn't be scared by anything.

Just ask Jim Fregosi. He made his big-league debut for the Los Angeles Angels in September 1961. He went 0-for-3 in his debut September 14 against Minnesota Twins left-hander Jim Kaat. In his next start September 22, he went 0-for-2 against Detroit Tigers right-hander Frank Lary. In his third start on September 23, he went 0-for-3 with three strikeouts against Bunning.

"I called my mother and said, 'I'll be home soon,'" Fregosi said.

Fregosi played 18 seasons in the majors and made six All-Star teams. He would face Bunning 15 more times in his career. He would manage just three hits (one of them a home run) to finish with a .176 average against him.

Pitcher Jim Bunning poses for a portrait prior to a 1966 game against the Cincinnati Reds at Crosley Field in Cincinnati, Ohio.

"He was nasty," Fregosi said. "I tell you what, it was a day's work when you had to face him."

Bunning, who was inducted into the Hall of Fame in 1996, could be a mean dude on the mound. He would knock people down. He would intimidate with his stare.

"His competitive nature was as good as you could ever have," said Clay Dalrymple, who caught Bunning from 1964 to 1967 with the Phillies. "When he walked onto the mound he was wound up as tight as you could wind up a guy to win. And that's one of the reasons he was very successful. If everybody walked out there with that attitude, there would be better pitching, believe me."

Bunning pitched just six seasons with the Phillies and won 89 games. He ranks sixth in franchise history with 1,197 strikeouts and ninth amongst Phillies pitchers who threw 1,000 or more innings with a 2.93 ERA. But from 1964 to 1967 few were better. He went 19–8 with a 2.63 ERA in 1964, 19–9 with a 2.60 ERA in 1965, 19–14 with a 2.41 ERA in 1966, and 17–15 with a 2.29 ERA in 1967. He would have won more games in '67, except he lost five 1–0 games.

In that four-year stretch, Bunning ranked third in the majors with 74 wins. Only Juan Marichal (82) and Kaat (76) had more. He also led baseball in strikeouts (992) and shutouts (23), ranked fourth with a 2.48 ERA and sixth in complete games (60). Oh, he also hit 58 batters, 11 more than famous Los Angeles Dodgers intimidator Don Drysdale.

"Let me just put it this way, my heart was always there, but my ass was never there," Fregosi said of his at-bats against Bunning.

"I remember we played a game in Montreal one time, in old Jarry Park," said Larry Bowa, who played with Bunning from 1970 to 1971. "And the Expos had Ron Hunt, the guy who loved to get hit. Well, Bunning threw him a sidearm curveball, Hunt never moved, and it hit him. The ball rolled toward the mound, and Bunning picked it up. He looked right at Hunt and he said, 'Ron, you want to get hit? I'll hit you next time.' And next time up, *bam*. Fastball. Drilled him right in the ribs. And he said to Hunt, 'OK, now you can go to first base.'"

Bunning had a sidearm delivery that proved terribly tough for right-handed batters, who hit just .229 against him compared to .257 for left-handed hitters.

"He had a great slider that just kept moving across the plate," Dalrymple said. "It didn't go down. It would come into the strike zone and slide out of the strike zone. He'd get a lot of hitters swinging at that for third strikes or maybe hitting the ball weakly because they couldn't reach it. He had a good curveball. It wasn't a quick breaker. It was a fairly big one. And his fastball he could move in and out. It tailed a little bit if you threw it into the right-hander, which was good because the slider would break the other way, which would offset that. One would break one way, and the other would break the other way."

Dalrymple said he had caught pitchers with better stuff than Bunning, who threw a perfect game on Father's Day in 1964, but nobody came to the ballpark more determined to win.

"I never saw Jim ever walk out there and not take at least some very decent stuff with him," he said. "I've caught other pitchers like Jim Palmer, and I walk out there and say, 'Holy cow, this isn't the Jim Palmer I know.' The fastball isn't there. The curveball isn't there. There's nothing there. He can't throw a strike. And the next time he'll throw a two-hitter."

Bunning never had those this-isn't-the-Jim-Bunning-I-know days.

"I missed a ground ball at the old Connie Mack Stadium one time," Bowa said. "And he stared a hole right through me. It felt like two piercing swords through my chest. But I don't think he did it to show me up."

He didn't. Dalrymple recalls the rare occasions when Bunning would give up runs in critical situations and he would return to the dugout and try to take out his frustrations on somebody, usually Dalrymple.

"He'd yell hard at me a couple times," he said. "I'd say, 'Jim, I'm on the same team you're on.' And that would settle him down. He had a great personality. He was a good family man. So you know when somebody says something that is supposed to shake you up or hurt your feelings that it's coming from the competitive side of him."

His competitiveness helped make him one of the five best starting pitchers in Phillies history.

Curt Schilling
1992–2000

Maybe Curt Schilling came a little too prepared to Game 1 of the 1993 World Series.

He had studied the tapes. He had memorized the strengths and weaknesses of Toronto Blue Jays hitters like Paul Molitor, Joe Carter, and Roberto Alomar. He had mapped out strategies for them. He had planned the types of pitches he would throw and when and where he would throw them. He had everything figured out.

And then he got rocked.

He allowed seven runs in six and a third innings in an 8–5 loss to the Toronto Blue Jays.

"I didn't see my outfielders' faces for six innings," Schilling said. "I think I found these guys' strengths. But now I've faced them, so this time I'll pitch to my strengths instead of to their weaknesses. Maybe I overanalyzed their hitters, I don't know."

Schilling redeemed himself immeasurably in Game 5 in a performance Phillies fans won't forget. It's the game that established Schilling as one of the best postseason pitchers in baseball history. The Phillies entered Game 5 on the brink of elimination, trailing the Blue Jays 3–1 in the best-of-seven Series. The Blue Jays had scored 25 runs in victories over the Phillies in Games 3 and 4, but Schilling quickly turned the tables. He allowed just five hits and three walks and struck out six in a brilliant shutout at Veterans Stadium to push the Series to Game 6 in Toronto.

"I wanted the ball," Schilling said. "I wanted the responsibility. I've said before, if you don't want the ball in these situations, why show up? You want your teammates to count on you at times like this."

From that point on, they knew they could count on him.

"He's gonna have to build a bigger garage," Darren Daulton said that night. "He's gonna need it to put a couple more Lamborghinis in it—'cause that guy's gonna make a hell of a lot of money before he's done. That right there was the Curt Schilling Show. He's turned into a big-time, big-game pitcher."

Daulton had no idea how big. Schilling deserves to be in any discussion about the best postseason pitchers in baseball history. He deserves to be included among names like Bob Gibson, Herb Pennock, Lefty Gomez, Johnny Podres, Orel Hershiser, John Smoltz, and Jim Palmer. In 19 postseason starts in his career with Philadelphia, Arizona, and Boston, Schilling is 11–2 with a 2.23 ERA. In Game 1 of the National League Championship Series against the Atlanta Braves in 1993, Schilling allowed seven hits,

Pitcher Curt Schilling tips his hat to the crowd on October 21, 1993, after defeating the Toronto Blue Jays 2–0 in Game 5 of the 1993 World Series. Schilling pitched a complete game shutout to move the Series back to Toronto for Game 6. Photo courtesy of AP Images.

two runs, and two walks and struck out 10 in eight innings. He would have picked up the win, except Mitch Williams blew a save in the ninth before the Phillies won 4–3 in 10 innings. In Game 5 of the NLCS, Schilling allowed four hits, two runs (one earned run), and three walks and struck out nine in eight-plus innings. He was in line for the win again when he walked Jeff Blauser to start the ninth inning and Ron Gant reached on an error to put runners on first and second with nobody out. With the Phillies holding a 3–0 lead, Williams blew another save and allowed the Braves to tie it. The Phillies won that game 4–3 in 10 innings.

In two starts in the NLCS, Schilling struck out 19 batters in 16 innings and had a 1.69 ERA. He struggled in Game 1 of the World Series before throwing his masterpiece in Game 5. In four postseason starts for the Phillies, Schilling is 1–1 with a 2.59 ERA. That compares pretty favorably to the other pitchers in this dream rotation. Grover Cleveland Alexander went 1–1 with a 1.53 ERA in the 1915 World Series for the Phillies. Robin Roberts went 0–1 with a 1.64 ERA in the 1950 World Series for the Phillies. Steve Carlton went 6–5 with a 3.33 ERA in 13 postseason starts for the Phillies. (Bunning never pitched in the postseason during his 17-year career.)

Schilling didn't have all of his best years with the Phillies, but he ranks sixth in franchise history with 101 wins. Carlton (241), Roberts (234), Alexander (190), Chris Short (132), and Curt Simmons (115) have more. He also ranks fourth with 1,554 strikeouts and 13th with a 3.35 ERA. He struck out a franchise single-season record 319 batters in 1997. He pitched on a series of terrible teams after '93 and ultimately begged his way out of Philadelphia. The Phillies traded him to the Arizona Diamondbacks on July 26, 2000, for Travis Lee, Vicente Padilla, Omar Daal, and Nelson Figueroa. He won a World Series with the Diamondbacks in 2001. He won two more World Series with the Red Sox in 2004 and 2007.

But as much as Schilling thought he prepared too much and overanalyzed for Game 1 of the World Series in '93, his exhaustive preparation before each start helped make him great. He had thousands of notebook pages and computer files detailing his experiences with every hitter he had faced when he pitched for the Phillies.

"If I get a hitter to swing at a 1-and-2 splitter, it's not because I'm lucky,"' he said. "It's because I'm prepared."

He even kept a book on umpires.

"They're human," he explained. "They have tendencies, just like pitchers and hitters. If it's the seventh inning and I have a 1-and-2 count and I look to freeze a hitter inside, I better know that the umpire is a guy who'll call that pitch. If he's not, I haven't prepared properly. I'm never going to be in the Hall of Fame. But I have a chance to be one of the best of my era. That and a World Series ring are what I want most. The best way to achieve those things is to be prepared for every start."

That preparation helped him become one of the best pitchers of his era. It also helped him win three World Series rings.

And that just might be enough to get him into the Hall of Fame.

The Closer
Tug McGraw
1975–84

Tug McGraw called it a Jack Daniel's trade.

He figured the front offices of the New York Mets and Phillies had to be loaded to make the trade they made December 3, 1974, when the Mets shipped McGraw, Don Hahn, and Dave Schneck to the Phillies for Del Unser, John Stearns, and Mac Scarce. That's how teams sometimes handled business then. They'd talk during the day, hit the hotel bar at night, and hash out a trade at 3:00 in the morning.

Drunk? Sober as a judge? Who knows? We only know the Phillies got tipsy after their champagne celebration October 21, 1980, after McGraw struck out Willie Wilson for the final out to win the Phillies' first World Series. It was one of the biggest saves in Phillies history, which is one reason why McGraw is the closer on this dream team. McGraw is fourth in Phillies history with 94 saves, pitching in an era that didn't use closers like they use them today. Only Jose Mesa (112), Steve Bedrosian (103), and Mitch

Williams (102) have more saves than McGraw. He ranks third in Phillies history with 463 games pitched behind Robin Roberts (529) and Steve Carlton (499). He ranks first with 313 games finished. He made the All-Star team with the Phillies in 1975. He finished fifth in Cy Young voting in 1980, when he went 5–4 with a 1.46 ERA and 20 saves. He received MVP votes in 1977 and 1980. He also went 2–3 with a 2.64 ERA and five saves in 18 postseason appearances for the Phillies.

"If I'm going to build a team, I'm going to get somebody that no matter what kind of team you have, if you can get into the ninth inning with a lead and you can close the game out and your team knows you can close the game out, you've got a chance to win some games," former Phillies manager Dallas Green said. "But if you bust your ass for eight innings and play and come back and finally get a lead and run somebody out there who can't close the game, there's nothing more demoralizing to a team than that."

McGraw was a man who could close games. He was a man his teammates believed in.

There have been Phillies closers with better individual seasons than McGraw, but it's tough to argue they had longer, more successful careers. Bedrosian won the NL Cy Young Award in 1987, when he went 5–3 with a 2.83 ERA and 40 saves. Jim Konstanty won the NL MVP in 1950, when he went 16–7 with a 2.66 ERA and 22 saves. Al Holland went 8–4 with a 2.26 ERA and 25 saves in 1983, finishing sixth for Cy Young and ninth for MVP. Billy Wagner went 4–3 with a 1.51 ERA and 38 saves in 2005. Mesa went 7–9 with a 2.67 ERA and 87 saves in 2001–02. Williams picked up 43 saves in 1993. Brad Lidge went 48-for-48 in save opportunities in 2008, including the postseason.

But there was more to McGraw than just his ability to close games. He had personality. He had fun. And it made him one of the most enduring and popular athletes in Philadelphia history. He named his pitches. He threw the Peggy Lee to batters on a 3–0 count. It was a meatball down the heart of the plate, the type of pitch hitters dream about. But they got so excited at the sight of the pitch they often grounded out or popped out, which caused them to say, "Is that all there is?" McGraw painted the corners with his four-seam fastball, and on occasion he'd change speeds to give it a little movement. He called that the Bo Derek because it had a nice tail on it. He would throw the John Jameson, which was hard and straight. He would throw his Cutty Sark, a cut fastball that would sail.

He never wanted to throw the Frank Sinatra, but he did. The Sinatra was a "Fly Me to the Moon" pitch that landed in the bleachers.

"That was usually a postdelivery name, instead of a predelivery name," he said. "I never meant to throw the Sinatra!"

The John Jameson. The Bo Derek. The Peggy Lee.

Beautiful.

"I think Tug attracted fans through sheer personality," Bill Giles said at McGraw's retirement news conference on February 14, 1985. "He just had this sincere enthusiasm, like your 12-year-old son playing Little League. To him, every game was like that 12-year-old kid hitting a grand slam. You could see it in his reactions and in the way he went about everything he did. Just the way he walked in from the bullpen was different."

McGraw retired after a 19-year career with the Mets and Phillies with 180 saves. At the time, only seven pitchers in baseball history had more saves than him: Rollie Fingers (324), Bruce Sutter (260), Sparky Lyle (238), Goose Gossage (231), Hoyt Wilhelm (227), Roy Face (193), and Mike Marshall (188). Only eight pitchers had appeared in more games than McGraw's 824.

Phillies fans don't remember those numbers. They remember 1980. McGraw came off the disabled list in July and allowed just three earned runs the rest of the way. In those final 33 regular-season appearances, he went 5–1 with a 0.52 ERA and 13 saves.

"That was actually the beginning of the end," McGraw said. "After that, I started having all the arm trouble. All that wear and tear on my arm (down the stretch) had to take its toll. But it was worth it."

It was. Nobody will ever forget the image of him raising his arms after he delivered the final out in Game 6.

"I was a hardworking guy," he said. "If I screwed up, I took my lumps and came back the next time. Philadelphia's a hardworking city. They appreciated that.... And I wasn't going to be a part of their bad day. I was going to be a part of their good one. And I think they appreciated that. Maybe it was because I wear my heart on my sleeve. If everybody did it, it would get old. But I just happened to be on a couple of teams where I was the exception.... I just showed my enjoyment different than other people. That doesn't mean that the others didn't enjoy it. I'm just a ham. You need some of those steady, level-headed guys to relate to. Just like you need some idiots to relate to."

THE LINEUPS

We have our Dream Team, but we need our lineup.

But for those folks screaming that Chuck Klein or Johnny Callison should have been in right field over Bobby Abreu, or Darren Daulton should have been behind the plate over Bob Boone, we figured we would have others fill out the lineup card. And who would be more qualified to fill out a lineup card than Phillies managers? But not just any Phillies managers. Managers who took their teams to the postseason. There have been seven managers in franchise history who have led the Phillies to the playoffs: Pat Moran (1915), Eddie Sawyer (1950), Danny Ozark (1976–78), Dallas Green (1980–81), Paul Owens (1983), Jim Fregosi (1993), and Charlie Manuel (2007–09).

We asked four managers from that group—Ozark, Green, Fregosi, and Manuel—to make their personal lineups for our personal Dream Team. We also asked them to pick one starting pitcher out of our five-man rotation that they would want on the mound for Game 7 of the World Series.

And because we know managers have strong opinions, we also gave them a wild-card selection. They could replace one player from the starting eight with any player they wanted for any reason they wished. They want Dick Allen at third instead of Mike Schmidt? They could do that. They want Lenny Dykstra in center instead of Richie Ashburn? They could do that. They want Steve

Jeltz at shortstop instead of Jimmy Rollins? OK, let's not get crazy, folks. They *can't* do that.

So here's how Ozark, Green, Fregosi, and Manuel filled out their lineup cards for arguably the greatest team in Phillies history:

Danny Ozark
1973–79
594–510 (.538)

Danny Ozark arrived from the Los Angeles Dodgers, where he served as Walter Alston's third-base coach for the previous eight seasons. He went 594–510 with the Phillies, which included three straight National League East championships from 1976 to 1978. His 594 victories are second-best in Phillies history behind only Gene Mauch, who was 645–684 in nine seasons.

Ozark arguably piloted the deepest and most talented teams in Phillies history. The Phillies went 101–61 in 1976 and 1977 but were swept in the National League Championship Series by the Cincinnati Reds in '76 and lost 3–1 in the best-of-five series to the Dodgers in '77.

He helped nurture some of the greatest talents in Phillies history, but he is forever linked to Black Friday in Game 3 of the '77 NLCS when he left Greg Luzinski in left field instead of using Jerry Martin as a defensive replacement, which he had done the entire season. The Phillies lost Game 3, partially because Luzinski couldn't make a catch in left in the ninth inning. The Phillies lost the series the next day.

Here is how Ozark filled out his lineup card before he died in 2009:

1. **Pete Rose, 1B**—"I'm absolutely leading him off. He gets hits. He's got the bat with the glass eye that knows where to hit the ball. He'd be perfect in the leadoff spot on this team."
2. **Jimmy Rollins, SS**—"I think he's one of the best hitters on the club. I think he can do a lot."
3. **Chase Utley, 2B**—"He can take pitches. He can pull the ball with a man on second base. He's just a great hitter."
4. **Mike Schmidt, 3B**—"He struck out a lot in my first year in '73, but it didn't bother him too much. But he obviously

became one of the best third basemen in history. He's a natural cleanup hitter on this team."

5. **Greg Luzinski**, LF—"It's difficult because you've got to have one guy backing up another guy. You've got Schmitty, a right-handed hitter. You've got Bull, a right-handed hitter. Then I've got Abreu following Greg."

6. **Bobby Abreu**, RF—"They would probably be pitching around Bull and he'd have the opportunity to hit. He's in the category of a .300 hitter. We've got five guys in this lineup that can probably hit .300, and he's one of them. And we've got power. It would be Halloween for some of the pitchers starting against us. They'd be scared."

7. **Bob Boone**, C—"Bobby made contact. He didn't strike out very much. You could hit and run with him. You could do a lot of things. He's not a speed ball, but when you're making contact at the right times you can do things with a hitter like that."

8. **Steve Carlton**, P—"Carlton can bunt guys over, and he's not too bad of a hitter."

9. **Richie Ashburn**, CF—"He's a Hall of Famer. He could be my leadoff man, but he's going to get on base for Utley and Schmitty. That's not a disgrace for him being down there. With Ashburn hitting ninth, you've got Rose coming up after him. You can hit and run with them a lot. Pete's going to hit the ball a lot, which is going to allow Ashburn to steal. It would be an interesting lineup."

Ozark used his wild card to replace Ryan Howard with Rose. Ozark liked Howard's power, but he didn't like his strikeouts. And who can argue against replacing a prodigious home-run hitter with baseball's Hit King? Rose made the 1980 team go, and Rose certainly would make this lineup go.

Ozark also chose Carlton to pitch his Must-Win Game with Robin Roberts a close second.

"It's tough, but I would take Lefty," he said. "But I would follow with Roberts. Robin gets the ball over the plate. He's a power pitcher. He controls the opposition. He would give up a few hits, but he won't walk anybody. If you walk four guys in the game that's four base hits. When you don't walk anybody that means you're not pitching from the stretch too often. That makes a big difference. Lefty has the power. He has the good breaking ball. He has the good move to first base. He's a good hitter. He had such a great year in '72, and he really had only one bad year when I was there in '73. Otherwise he was outstanding. And he's a hell of a competitor. But so is Robbie. He'd never throw the towel in. He might give up five runs, but he knew he had eight guys out there chasing the ball, so he let them help him out."

Dallas Green
1979–81
169–130 (.565)

Dallas Green stood in the middle of the Carpenter Complex in Clearwater, Florida, in February 2004, when somebody asked him about the Phillies' chances of winning another World Series. The Phillies had just added Billy Wagner, Eric Milton, and Tim Worrell to their roster, so hopes were high considering they already had one of the more potent offenses in the National League.

Green said he liked their chances, although he offered a reminder that it's incredibly difficult to go all the way.

"If it were easy, I wouldn't be the only son of a bitch wearing a ring," he said.

Green piloted the Phillies to their first world championship in 1980, but it was a love-hate relationship between him and his players. He criticized them. He yelled at them. They didn't like it. But guess what? The team came together and won.

"I was a prick to a degree. That's what the guys called me. Until they got that," he said, looking at the championship ring on his hand.

Green is one of the most iconic figures in Philadelphia sports history because of that magical season. Here is his lineup card:

1. **Richie Ashburn**, CF—"Whitey probably is the best bat-control guy on the team and one of the fastest guys in baseball, so he belongs in the No. 1 slot."

2. **Chase Utley**, 2B—"Utley has got power. He's a left-handed hitter, obviously, so he's going to shoot for the hole. Or he's smart enough and intelligent enough to let a ball go through if Ashburn is stealing. He's an ideal second hitter."
3. **Greg Luzinski**, LF—"Luzinski is a power guy, also a high-average guy. He's going to drive runs in, and that's what he's paid to do."
4. **Mike Schmidt**, 3B—"I think Schmitty is an ideal fourth guy for the simple reason that he has power, he can hit for a high average, and believe it or not he has speed. So if we go 1-2-3 in the first, we've got a guy leading off the next inning that conceivably could help score a run as well."
5. **Ryan Howard**, 1B—"I dropped Howard into the fifth hole behind Schmidt, just because he strikes out too much and he's not going to run, so if we go 1-2-3, I don't like Howard leading off the next inning."

Phillies manager Dallas Green (center) puts his arm around relief pitcher Tug McGraw (No. 45) as shortstop Larry Bowa (right) comes out to offer his congratulations after the Phillies won the 1980 World Series 4–3 in Kansas City on October 19, 1980. Photo courtesy of AP Images.

6. **Pete Rose**, RF—"Rose is my right fielder. He's played right field. He's played all positions, and he's one of the best baseball players I've ever been around. He belongs in this lineup. He'd probably get mad for being down that low, but I think that's where he belongs in this lineup."

7. **Jimmy Rollins**, SS—"Rollins is kind of the same thing as Pete. But down there we at least have some speed. We have some bat potential as well. So Rollins is my seventh hitter."

8. **Bob Boone**, C—"Boonie is bringing up the rear, mainly because I think he's a better breaking-ball hitter than Rollins and he's going to get some breaking balls because the pitcher is hitting behind him."

9. **Steve Carlton**, P—"Steve is one of my favorite favorites of all time. If you look at his statistics, he belongs on top of the list, in my opinion."

Green, like Ozark, chose Rose as his wild-card selection, but he put him in right field to replace Bobby Abreu. Green also lined up the Dream Team rotation, which included Grover Cleveland Alexander, Robin Roberts, Jim Bunning, and Curt Schilling. He made Carlton his Game 7 starter.

"I obviously don't know Alexander at all other than reading the stats, but I put him second mainly because back in his day there was no question that there were no peers," Green said. "Robbie is right behind him for the same reason. I don't think he had many peers in his era as well. Bunning, I played with him. I know he's got heart and I know he's got great stuff. He's one of the best competitors that I've ever been around. And Schilling probably doesn't belong down that low, but there's no place to put him except fifth. Schill, I loved him because of his competitiveness and he's a big-game pitcher. I've always had a great feeling for Schill."

Jim Fregosi
1991–96
431–463 (.482)

Jim Fregosi managed the worst team in the National League East in 1992, when the Phillies went 70–92. They went 97–65 in 1993 to not only win the NL East, but the NL pennant before losing to the Toronto Blue Jays in six memorable games in the World Series.

Fregosi led a cast of characters that included Lenny Dykstra, John Kruk, Mitch Williams, Dave Hollins, and Curt Schilling. That group fit the city of Philadelphia perfectly, which is why the '93 squad is one of the most popular teams in Philadelphia sports history.

Here is Fregosi's lineup:

1. **Richie Ashburn**, CF—"Richie always was a leadoff hitter and these other guys can hit anyplace."
2. **Jimmy Rollins**, SS—"He can run. He's a switch-hitter sitting behind a left-handed hitter."
3. **Chase Utley**, 2B—"I like Utley there because he hits for average and he hits for power."
4. **Mike Schmidt**, 3B—"Schmidt is one of the greatest home-run hitters of all time."
5. **Ryan Howard**, 1B—"To give Schmidt a little protection, I'm going to hit Howard behind him. If he just played the month of September, what a career he would have."
6. **Greg Luzinski**, LF—"You want to have a right-hander hitter behind Howard to split it up."
7. **Darren Daulton**, C—"I want Daulton here to protect Luzinski. Boonie was a great player, but Boonie was never the offensive threat that Daulton was. I mean, Daulton led the league in RBIs one year as a catcher. I'm just a little prejudiced toward Daulton because he played for me, and he was quite a leader on the club. This isn't anything against Boone."
8. **Bobby Abreu**, RF—"And, hey, Abreu is hitting eighth. We'll get him on base so the pitcher can bunt him over."
9. **Curt Schilling**, P—"These guys are all great pitchers, but Schilling just pitched so good in the postseason. And he did that pitching for me, so I'm a little biased that way."

Fregosi had a choice to make: take Daulton over Bob Boone at catcher or Lenny Dykstra over Ashburn in center field. He chose Daulton, although Fregosi has an affinity for Dykstra. Dykstra had the best season for a center fielder in modern Phillies history in 1993, when he hit .305 with 19 homers, 66 RBIs, 143 runs, and 129 walks. Meanwhile, Ashburn is one of just two players in baseball history to have more than 550 at-bats in a season and 20 or fewer RBIs. He had 20 RBIs in 564 at-bats in 1959. Morrie Rath had 19 RBIs in 591 at-bats for the Chicago White Sox in 1912.

Fregosi also set up his rotation. He chose Schilling first for his big-game ability. He is 11–2 with a 2.23 ERA in 19 postseason starts. Steve Carlton, who slides into the second slot, is 6–6 with a 3.26 ERA in 16 playoff appearances. Falling behind Schilling and Carlton were Robin Roberts, Jim Bunning, and Grover Cleveland Alexander.

Charlie Manuel
2005–Present
447–363 (.552)

Charlie Manuel brought October baseball to Phillies fans for the first time in 14 years when he guided the Phillies to one of the greatest comebacks in baseball history in 2007. He trumped that memorable year when he led the Phillies to their second World Series championship in 2008 and to their second consecutive trip to the World Series in 2009.

Here is his lineup:

1. **Richie Ashburn**, CF—"Whitey was a guy that had tremendous bat control. He hit for a high average. He got on base a lot. He had good speed. He's a left-hander. In his day he was a tremendous leadoff hitter."

2. **Jimmy Rollins**, SS—"One of the reasons I've got him hitting second is because of his speed and he can switch-hit. And one of the biggest things about him is that he can hook the hole on the right side of the diamond. I think that's one of his pluses as a left-handed hitter. He's got a short, quick swing. He pulls the ball strong."

3. **Chase Utley**, 2B—"I've got Utley hitting third because he's consistent. He puts the ball in play. He puts up good enough power numbers to hit in that hole."

Manager Charlie Manuel addresses the fans as he celebrates the Phillies' 4–3 win over the Tampa Bay Rays to win the 2008 World Series during the continuation of Game 5 on October 29, 2008, at Citizens Bank Park.

4. **Mike Schmidt**, 3B—"Schmidt is hitting fourth because I want to split up Utley and Howard. Having Schmidt in the four-hole gives you a lot of balance right there in the middle of the lineup."

5. **Ryan Howard**, 1B—"Howard is fifth and Luzinski is sixth. Bull plays a big role where Howard hits because of the balance in our lineup."

6. **Greg Luzinski**, LF—"I saw Bull when he was 17 in the instructional league and I played against him when he was in Triple A in Eugene. I saw him play his whole career. He was a tremendous hitter, a high-average hitter for a big guy. He didn't get many leg hits. That means he's putting the ball in play and he's hitting the ball hard. He was a good player."

7. **Bobby Abreu**, RF—"He's probably one of the best seven-hole hitters you'll ever have. He's a high on-base-percentage guy. He can steal anywhere from 25 to 50 bags. I'd say the seven hole might take some RBIs away from him, but at the same time he can be very productive in this spot because he is a high on-base-percentage guy."

8. **Bob Boone**, C—"That would let Boone swing the bat more than just sacrifice bunt and stuff. That means you don't have to hit-and-run with your eight-hole hitter. That leaves Carlton to hit ninth, and he can bunt guys over."

9. **Steve Carlton**, P—"I saw Bunning pitch at the end of his career. He was a tremendous pitcher. I obviously didn't see Alexander, but I've always heard how good he was. I've seen Bunning and Roberts. Both of them were very good. It was very close. Carlton, Bunning, and Roberts—if you pick any one of them, I don't think you could go wrong. But because I had to pick one I picked Carlton. And I picked Carlton because I hit against him. He had a tremendous fastball and he had a lights-out slider. His command was good. He always commanded the ball real low in the strike zone."

Manuel didn't use his wild card, although he said he thought long and hard about finding a spot for Rose.

"The fact that I had Bobby Abreu might have played a role in that because he plays the role that Rose plays," Manuel said. "But Pete Rose was one of my favorite players. He's one of the greatest players to ever play the game. It's tough. Pete could play left, third, second, right, first. He could play different positions. I definitely thought of him. But I think that lineup there gives us the best balanced lineup we could have. If you look, I've got left-switch-left-right-left-right-left-right. That's pretty good. Abreu hits left-handers pretty good. So does Utley. Howard, he hits for power against left-handers."

Power. High average. Speed. What's not to like?

THE MOVES THEY MADE

OLD PETE FOR PICKLES

If you're looking for the moment the Phillies went from respectable to laughingstock in the early 20th century, from solid to utter mess, look no further than the trade Phillies owner William Baker made December 11, 1917.

Baker sent Hall of Fame pitcher Grover Cleveland Alexander and catcher Bill Killefer to the Chicago Cubs for pitcher Mike Prendergast, catcher Pickles Dillhoefer, and $60,000. Alexander had won 190 games for the Phillies in his first seven seasons in the majors. He went 31–10 with a 1.22 ERA in 1915. He threw a major-league-record 16 shutouts in 1916, when he went 33–12 with a 1.55 ERA. He went 30–13 with a 1.83 ERA in 1917. He led the league in wins and strikeouts from 1914 to 1917. He led the league in shutouts from 1915 to 1917. He dominated.

Baker traded him anyway. He feared losing Alexander to the draft as the United States entered World War I.

He also had another reason to trade him.

"I needed the money," Baker said.

Alexander pitched three games in 1918, served in France, and returned in 1919 to continue his successful career. He finished his career with 373 wins, which is tied for third in history with Christy Mathewson. Prendergast and Dillhoefer? Prendergast went 13–14 with a 2.89 ERA in 1918. He made just five appearances in 1919 and never pitched in the majors again. Dillhoefer

Grover Cleveland Alexander winds up for a pitch, circa 1910s.

had just one hit in 11 at-bats in eight games for the Phillies in 1918. The Phillies traded him to the St. Louis Cardinals in January 1919, and he never played in the majors after 1921. Baker would continue to sell his top talent for cash and little talent in return until he died after the 1930 season.

But the Alexander trade set in motion an incredible run of futility that lasted until 1950.

FERGIE TO THE CUBS

The Phillies suffered a historic collapse in 1964 but never had the chance to blow any leads in 1965.

They finished in sixth place at 85–76. Phillies general manager John Quinn and manager Gene Mauch tried to improve in 1966 by adding veteran arms to pitch behind Jim Bunning and Chris Short. They wanted reliability, but to get that reliability they needed to move young talent. They moved one of the best. They traded Ferguson Jenkins, first baseman John Herrnstein, and center fielder Adolfo Phillips to the Chicago Cubs on April 21, 1966, for pitchers Larry Jackson and Bob Buhl. Jackson was a former 20-game winner in the twilight of his career. He went 15–13 in 1966, 13–15 in 1967, and 13–17 in 1968—his final season in the majors. Buhl also was in the twilight of his career. He went 6–8 in 32 appearances for the Phillies in 1966. He made just three appearances in 1967 and never pitched in the majors again.

Jenkins? The Hall of Famer made 60 appearances (12 starts) for the Cubs in 1966, before they converted him into a full-time starter in 1967. He went 20–13 with a 2.80 ERA. It began a streak of six-straight 20-win seasons for the Cubs. He won 20 or more games in seven of his first eight seasons after the trade—the seventh time coming with the Texas Rangers in 1974 when he went 25–12. Jenkins went 284–226 with a 3.34 ERA in his 19-year career. He won the Cy Young Award in 1971 and is the only pitcher in baseball history to have more than 3,000 strikeouts and fewer than 1,000 walks.

"I never got the feeling from Mauch that he thought I had the guts to be a successful pitcher," Jenkins said.

Bob Uecker joined the Phillies as a catcher in 1966. Uecker recalled how Mauch took him around in spring training and told him a little about each pitcher.

"See that guy over there? That's Ray Culp," Mauch said. "And that's Fergie Jenkins. We don't think he can win in the big leagues as a starter."

"I don't even know him," Uecker recalled. "So I'm like, 'That's OK with me. I don't think he can win with me as a starter, either.'"

"I always got a lot of satisfaction out of beating the Phillies after that," Jenkins said. "I never really had any bad feelings about Mauch. In fact, we became good friends later on. He told me once his biggest mistake was not seeing my potential as a starting pitcher. He said he always thought of me in terms of a reliever, and to be honest I always thought I was a reliever until Robin Roberts took me under his wing in Chicago."

Roberts was finishing his career when Jenkins was beginning his. The Cubs signed Roberts as a free agent July 13, 1966, the day the Houston Astros released him. Roberts, who helped Cubs manager Leo Durocher as their pitching coach, studied Jenkins and figured he could be a successful starter.

"I kept watching Fergie warm up in the bullpen, and all I saw was a big guy who could throw hard and throw the ball where he wanted to," Roberts said. "He had a good slider and he threw everything down around the knees. He looked like a starting pitcher and he threw like a starting pitcher. Fergie always said he didn't think he had the stamina to be a starter, but I told him the way he throws he wouldn't need that much stamina."

Jenkins had the stamina to pitch 19 years in the majors to make that 1966 trade one of the worst in history.

A WISE MOVE FOR LEFTY

John Quinn didn't feel like he needed to explain himself, but he did anyway.

But explaining himself eventually turned into defending himself, and defending himself eventually turned into restraining himself. The Phillies general manager traded Rick Wise to the

St. Louis Cardinals for Steve Carlton on February 25, 1972, and one would have thought he shipped Mike Schmidt in his prime to the New York Mets for a six-pack of Old Milwaukee.

Wise for Carlton bothered many people in Philadelphia. Wise had thrown a no-hitter (and hit two homers in the same game) for the Phillies in 1971, the highlight of an otherwise awful 67–95 season. He went 17–14 with a 2.88 ERA. He made the All-Star team. He was just 26. But Wise wanted more money from the Phillies and the Phillies weren't going to budge. They were at an impasse. The St. Louis Cardinals found themselves in a similar situation with Carlton. Carlton wanted $65,000 for the 1972 season. Cardinals owner Gussie Busch only wanted to pay him $55,000.

Based on a $10,000 difference, the beer baron decided to trade Carlton. The Phillies jumped at the opportunity.

"I was like, in shock," Carlton said. "I called [Cardinals general manager] Bing Devine back after he called me. I said, 'I'll take the money you offered me. I'll take anything.' It was a done deal by then."

Carlton knew the Phillies were bad. Perhaps that's why the Phillies couldn't believe their good fortune.

"I think Carlton is the top pitcher in the National League," Quinn told the *Philadelphia Inquirer* sportswriter Frank Dolson from the porch in the back of the Jack Tar Hotel in Clearwater, Florida. "This guy, in my opinion, is in the category of Warren Spahn."

Quinn's voice filled with anger as he said those words. He believed in Carlton, and he couldn't believe Dolson didn't understand. Carlton went 20–9 with the Cardinals in 1971, but Wise had earned hero status in Philadelphia. After he threw the no-hitter, Bill Giles tried to get people to Veterans Stadium by giving away thousands of pictures of Wise. He was a face of the franchise.

"It's elementary, elementary," Quinn said. "You have to trade a Rick Wise for a Steve Carlton. This guy's going to win 20 regardless of where he pitches. He was 20–9, not 17–14. I don't know how anyone can fault us. I just can't understand."

Finally Quinn, a staunch Republican, said, "It's like you had Lyndon Johnson and somebody else had Eisenhower, and you have a chance to make a trade. What would you do?"

Quinn took Ike. Carlton, who won 27 of the Phillies' 59 games in 1972, became arguably the greatest left-hander in baseball history, certainly entering the discussion with Spahn like Quinn suggested. Carlton won 329 games in his career. He struck out 4,136 batters. He won four Cy Youngs. He's in the Hall of Fame. Wise won 188 games in his career, pitching for five teams. He went a career-best 19–12 with a 3.95 ERA for the Boston Red Sox in 1975 but never reached the stratosphere of Carlton.

The Phillies had come out on top.

PETE ROSE WAY

Pete Rose knew he wouldn't play for Cincinnati in 1979. The Reds made that clear when they took the unusual step of placing an ad in a Cincinnati newspaper explaining their side in a salary dispute.

Rose was upset about the ad and knew it meant the end, but he also knew other teams would want him.

Who wouldn't want Pete Rose?

He already had a Hall of Fame résumé. He had more than 3,000 hits. He had helped the Reds win four National League pennants and two World Series. He had just finished making a run at Joe DiMaggio's 56-game hitting streak with a 44-game hitting streak in '78. He played hard, too. He once said he would "walk through hell in a gasoline suit to keep playing baseball." That attitude rubbed off on his teammates, and that's the type of player the Phillies felt they needed to get them over the top to win the World Series.

"We had a lot of basic talent, but we really didn't have a leader," Bill Giles said. "We didn't have somebody who had the confidence to chew out the other players. Pete was certainly a leader the way he played the game."

Rose would become a rich man on the free-agent market. Money wasn't the most important thing, but it was important because he considered himself the best player in baseball. And the best player in baseball should be paid like the best. Teams reflected that sentiment. The Kansas City Royals offered Rose a four-year,

Pete Rose slides headfirst into third base in March 1986 during spring training in Clearwater, Florida.

$4 million contract, plus an option and a stake in owner Ewing Kauffman's oil investments. The Atlanta Braves offered a three-year, $3 million contract, plus a yearly $100,000 pension that he would receive until he died. The St. Louis Cardinals couldn't offer the money the Royals and Braves offered, but owner Gussie Busch threw in a Budweiser beer distributorship to sweeten the deal. Pittsburgh Pirates owner John Galbreath's offer came in lower than other teams, but he offered Rose two brood mares, plus the stud services of his top horses.

But what would the Phillies offer? They were the team Rose really wanted to play for. He had become friends with Mike Schmidt and Larry Bowa and others over the years. He would have dinner with them when the Phillies were in Cincinnati. He admired the way they played. He knew they had a chance to win the World Series after winning the National League East in 1976, 1977, and 1978. The Phillies felt Rose was the player who could put them over the top. But as much as Rose wanted to be in

Philadelphia, he wouldn't play for free. So Rose and his agent, Reuven Katz, flew to Philadelphia on a private jet to meet with Phillies owner Ruly Carpenter and Giles.

Katz brought a highlight reel of Rose for the pair to watch.

"We don't want to see the video," Giles said. "We know what he is."

Katz then told Carpenter and Giles how great Rose is at marketing and how great he is with the media.

"Fine," Giles said. "We know that."

The foursome was about to have lunch, when Carpenter said, "Let's knock out the bull crap here. What kind of money do you want?"

Katz told Carpenter that he had received a four-year contract worth seven figures a year. Carpenter, a Yale graduate, started counting on his fingers because he wanted to make sure he heard what he heard. He couldn't believe it. He wanted Rose, but he wouldn't pay a million dollars a year for him. The Phillies had signed Mike Schmidt to a six-year, $3.3 million contract in 1977. That would be almost twice as much as what Schmidt was making.

"Let's have lunch," Carpenter said.

The Phillies later said they could pay Rose $600,000 a year over four years. There were no oil wells, no beer distributorships, no horses, no pensions. Just $2.4 million over four years. Rose couldn't take that. He couldn't. He wanted to play for the Phillies, but he couldn't take so much less than the Royals and Braves offered. Realizing no deal could be struck, the Phillies held a news conference telling reporters that Rose wouldn't be coming to Philadelphia. Giles drove Rose and Katz back to the airport. But before they arrived, Giles pulled out the National League's Green Book, the record book baseball distributes to teams and media. Giles, understanding Rose's ego and sense of baseball history, reminded Rose that if he went to the American League he would not be able to break the National League's all-time hits record, which Stan Musial held with 3,630.

"You're second or third in all these offensive categories," Giles said. "If you go to the American League, all your kids and grandkids are going to see that you're second and third. Don't you want to be first in all these categories?"

It struck a nerve with Rose. Before Rose got on the plane, Katz whispered to Giles that if he could get Carpenter to offer $800,000 per year, he probably could get Rose to sign with the Phillies. Giles went to WPHL-TV and asked them to kick in an extra $200,000 a year for broadcasting rights because Rose's arrival certainly would boost ratings and make them money. The station went for it. On December 5, 1978, the Phillies announced they had signed Rose to a four-year contract worth $810,000 per season that made him the highest-paid player in baseball.

Rose got his contract. The Phillies got their player.

"St. Louis wanted me to replace Lou Brock, and I didn't want to do that," Rose said. "Kansas City wanted me to change leagues, and I didn't want to do that. Ted Turner didn't care about my baseball ability. He said flat out, I want you to help me sell TV. And Pittsburgh, I didn't think they had a good enough team. But I thought the team sitting on the powder keg was the Phillies. They were the closest team to get where I wanted to be at that stage of my life and that was the World Series. And I was right, because I was there five years, played in two World Series and three playoffs."

GO AHEAD, TAKE SANDBERG

We have to have Sandberg to make this trade.
You have to have him?
Yeah, we have to have him.
Well, OK then. He's yours.

The Phillies traded Ryne Sandberg to the Chicago Cubs on January 27, 1982, not because they wanted to trade him, but because they wanted to trade Larry Bowa. They just needed to include Sandberg to make it happen. It turned out to be one of the worst trades in history. The Phillies got Ivan DeJesus. The Cubs got Bowa and Sandberg, a Hall of Fame second baseman.

Bowa had become embroiled in a bitter contract dispute with the new Phillies president Bill Giles. Bowa, who had just turned

36, wanted the three-year contract extension that owner Ruly Carpenter had promised him before he had sold the team. Giles had no plans to sign an aging shortstop to a contract extension, especially because the Phillies had top prospect Julio Franco coming through their farm system. So Bowa called Giles a liar. He said the organization had no class.

Bowa had to go. But where? Former Phillies manager Dallas Green had started to run the show in Chicago, and he had interest. But he said the only way he would send DeJesus to the Phillies was if they included Sandberg.

"We knew we had them over a barrel," Green said. "Giles had already made the mistake of telling the world Bowa was gone. I kept saying, 'Since we were the Little Sisters of the Poor, we had to get a plus in the trade.'"

The Phillies hemmed and hawed. They tried to expand the deal to include hard-throwing right-hander Lee Smith. But the Cubs didn't want players like Sparky Lyle, Don McCormack, and Del Unser in a package that included Smith. The Cubs wanted somebody like George Vukovich, and the Phillies were not about to trade him because they thought he had a bright future. Their dilemma with Sandberg was that they weren't sure what position he would play. Most didn't think he could play shortstop. They thought he could be a third baseman, except Mike Schmidt was there. They thought he could be a second baseman, except Manny Trillo was there. They thought maybe he could play one of the corner outfield positions. They even tried him as a center fielder, but that experiment was short-lived.

They never gave him a shot at any of those positions, and by the time Sandberg won National League Most Valuable Player honors in 1984, Franco, Trillo, and Vukovich (along with Jay Baller and Jerry Willard) had been traded to the Cleveland Indians in the 5-for-1 deal that got them Von Hayes.

"Sandberg is the biggest mistake we've made since I took over the operation of the ballclub," Giles said in '84. "We knew Ryne was going to be a good player, but he's become a great player."

Richie Ashburn had a revealing look at Sandberg's evaluation within the Phillies system in a November 15, 1984, column he

Ryne Sandberg practices in the batting cages before a game at Veterans Stadium during the 1981 season.

wrote for the *Philadelphia Daily News*. The Phillies let Ashburn peek at the team's scouting reports. The Phillies drafted Sandberg in the 20th round in 1978, and he hit .311 in 56 games for Helena. Phillies scout Bill Harper wrote in his reports that Sandberg did not have "much body bounce—he's a dead-ass type player." Another scout, W.H. "Moose" Johnson, wrote, "May be a little stiff, plays too shallow at shortstop, and will struggle with the bat for a while. His crouch stance makes him vulnerable to high, tight pitches, but he does stay tough at the plate." Minor-league instructor Larry Rojas looked more favorably upon Sandberg during his rookie-ball season. He wrote, "Sandberg doesn't say much, but has done a very good job offensively and defensively. He has good hands. He can steal a base almost anytime he wants. He's a line-drive-type hitter who hits the ball up the middle and to right-center field. I recommend him highly."

Sandberg seemed to be on his way, but he hit .247 for Single A Spartanburg in 1979. Former Phillies shortstop Granny Hamner, who worked for the Phillies as an instructor, called Sandberg a disappointment. Rojas seemed concerned, too. He wrote, "Am a little worried about his hitting—not handling the outside pitch well. I would like to see more drive and aggressiveness."

Bill Dancy, Sandberg's manager, said in July 1979 that he would want Sandberg at the plate in a clutch situation, but considered him a "chance prospect" in his final report. Spartanburg coach Mel Roberts said Sandberg "doesn't put much effort into what he's doing. Has a lot of ability that he has not come close to using this season. Has average attitude and desire. Below average in drive."

Sandberg hit .310 for Double A Reading in 1980 and .293 for Triple A Oklahoma City in 1981. Hamner changed his outlook on Sandberg. He called him a "definite major-league prospect," although he didn't think he could play a big-league shortstop. But in the end, the improved reports on Sandberg from Hamner and others weren't enough to convince the Phillies to keep him.

Ashburn wrote that Phillies vice president of player development Jim Baumer, minor-league executive secretary Bill Gargano, and assistant director of minor leagues and scouting Jack Pastore got upset when Phillies general manager Paul Owens said they included Sandberg in the trade for DeJesus because "our minor-league reports weren't that good on Sandberg."

The Phillies aren't the first team to trade a future stud. The Cubs traded Lou Brock to the St. Louis Cardinals for Ernie Broglio in 1964. The Boston Red Sox sent Jeff Bagwell to the Houston

Astros for Larry Andersen in 1990. The Detroit Tigers shipped John Smoltz to the Atlanta Braves for Doyle Alexander in 1997. The Seattle Mariners sent Derek Lowe and Jason Varitek to the Boston Red Sox for Heathcliff Slocumb in 1997.

Sandberg entered the Hall of Fame in 2005 after a remarkable 16-year career in which he won one MVP, made 10 All-Star teams, and won nine Gold Gloves and seven Silver Slugger Awards. Bowa played shortstop for the Cubs team that made the National League Championship Series in 1984. DeJesus? He hit no better than .257 in three seasons with the Phillies, who traded him and Bill Campbell to the St. Louis Cardinals for Dave Rucker in 1985.

It turns out Sandberg couldn't play shortstop. But he could play a heck of a second base.

HOW THEY BUILT THE '08 CHAMPS

A world championship team isn't built in a day. It takes years, and the 2008 Phillies were no exception.

The first piece came in 1996, when the Phillies selected Jimmy Rollins in the second round of the June amateur draft. The final piece came when the Phillies picked up outfielder Matt Stairs in a trade with the Toronto Blue Jays before the August 31 waiver trade deadline.

"It's been a long ride, I'll tell you that much," Rollins said the night the Phillies won the World Series. "But we did it. We did it. That part is over. That establishing that winning attitude in this organization has come to fruition. I've always said, you start back with Ed Wade and the way he drafted. They always said we were years away. Unfortunately, he wasn't here to see it out. But they did a great job at hiring a man like Pat Gillick who knows how to win and goes out and puts teams together."

Here is a look at how the Phillies built the 25-man roster that won the Phillies the World Series:

Pitchers

Joe Blanton (acquired from the Oakland A's on July 17, 2008, in exchange for Adrian Cardenas, Josh Outman, and Matt Spencer).

The Phillies lost the CC Sabathia sweepstakes and considered right-hander Rich Harden too risky to pursue because of his health history. So they acquired Blanton, who moved Adam Eaton out of the rotation for the rest of the season. Blanton went 4–0 with a 4.20 ERA in 13 regular-season starts (the Phillies were 9–4 in those starts) and 2–0 with a 3.18 ERA in three postseason starts. He also hit a home run in Game 4 of the World Series.

Clay Condrey (acquired from the San Diego Padres on March 28, 2004, for Trino Aguilar). A starter converted into a reliever in the minor leagues in 2006, Condrey went 3–4 with a 3.26 ERA in 56 appearances. It was Condrey's first full season in the majors after being shuttled back and forth from the majors to the minors, including four times in 2007.

Chad Durbin (signed as a free agent on December 20, 2007). The Detroit Tigers didn't offer Durbin a contract after the 2008 season, which made him a free agent. The Phillies signed him, thinking he could be a swing man—a long man in the bullpen who could start on occasion if necessary. He proved to be more valuable than that. He went 5–4 with a 2.87 ERA and one save in 71 appearances, leading National League relievers with 87⅔ innings pitched.

Scott Eyre (acquired from the Chicago Cubs on August 7, 2008, for prospect Brian Schlitter). The Phillies had been searching for a left-handed relief pitcher for some time. Thankfully for them, Eyre fell out of favor with Cubs manager Lou Piniella and became available. He went 3–0 with a 1.88 ERA in 19 appearances with the Phillies.

Cole Hamels (selected 17th overall in the first round of the June 2002 draft). The Phillies were told they took a risk drafting Hamels because he broke the humerus bone in his left arm in high school. The Phillies were undeterred, and it paid off. Hamels went 14–10 with a 3.09 ERA in 2008, setting a career high with 227⅓ innings pitched. But he saved his best for last. He went 4–0 with a 1.80 ERA in five postseason starts, earning NLCS MVP and World Series MVP honors.

J.A. Happ (selected in the third round of the June 2004 draft). Happ made the postseason roster as a long man. He went

1–0 with a 3.69 ERA in eight appearances (four starts) in the regular season.

Brad Lidge (acquired with Eric Bruntlett from the Houston Astros on November 7, 2007, for Michael Bourn, Geoff Geary, and Mike Constanzo). Lidge needed a change of scenery after a couple inconsistent seasons with Houston. The Phillies took a shot and struck gold. Lidge went 2–0 with a 1.95 ERA and 41 saves in 41 opportunities. He is only the second closer in baseball history to save more than 40 games in a season without blowing a save. He had a 0.96 ERA and seven saves in the postseason, too. "There's a lot of talk about smaller pick-ups," Gillick said. "The big pick-up was Lidge. I'm proud of that. What can you say? To go through the season and go through the playoffs and not blow a save? That's big. I'm as proud of him that after Houston he came over here and was as dominant as he was. If you want to take a big step, that was a big step."

Ryan Madson (selected in the ninth round of the June 1998 draft). Madson established himself as Lidge's setup man late in the season. He went 4–2 with a 3.05 ERA and one save in 76 appearances overall, but had a 0.63 ERA from August 31 through the end of the season.

Jamie Moyer (acquired with cash from the Seattle Mariners on August 19, 2006, for Andrew Baldwin and Andrew Barb). The Phillies held a fire sale at the July 31, 2006, non-waiver trade deadline but reversed course when they found themselves in the thick of the NL wild-card race a few weeks later. They got Moyer, who enjoyed pitching for his hometown team so much that he signed an extension after the season. "I grew up watching this silly team play," he said. "And now I'm standing in their clubhouse as a player and we won a world championship. Wow. World championship. That's the first time I've ever used those words. It sounds great."

Brett Myers (selected 12th overall in the first round of the June 1999 draft). Myers was considered the second-best high school pitcher in the draft behind Josh Beckett in 1999. He went from Opening Day starter to closer in 2007 and back to Opening Day starter in 2008. But he couldn't make the transition back to the rotation and pitched so poorly that the Phillies sent him to the minor leagues before the All-Star Break. He returned and went 7–2 with a 1.80 ERA in his 11 starts through the end of the regular season.

J.C. Romero (signed as a minor-league free agent June 22, 2007). The Boston Red Sox released him, but Romero received such scant interest on the open market that the Phillies signed him to a minor-league contract. He had a 1.24 ERA in 51 appearances in 2007, and a 2.75 ERA in 81 appearances in 2008.

Catchers

Chris Coste (signed as a minor-league free agent October 29, 2004). Nobody thought much about Coste when the Phillies signed him in 2004. Just another catcher/infielder. Just more inventory. But he proved he could hit. After finally making the majors in 2006, he made his first Opening Day roster in 2008 and hit .263 with nine homers and 36 RBIs.

Carlos Ruiz (signed as an amateur free agent December 4, 1998). The Phillies scouted Ruiz as an 18-year-old second baseman, but didn't think he had the quickness to play the infield. But they did like his arm and bat. They asked him to catch, he showed promise, and they signed him for $8,000. Ruiz, who hit just .219 during the regular season, hit .313 in the NLCS and .375 with one homer and three RBIs in the World Series, including knocking in the winning run in Game 3.

Infielders

Eric Bruntlett (acquired with Lidge from the Astros on November 7, 2007). The Phillies needed a utility infielder because Abraham Nunez wasn't coming back, so they asked the Astros to include Bruntlett in the Lidge trade. Bruntlett filled in for Rollins at shortstop early in the season and became Pat Burrell's defensive replacement in left field late in the season. He scored winning runs in Games 3 and 5 of the World Series.

Greg Dobbs (claimed off waivers January 15, 2007). The Mariners needed to make room on their 40-man roster for relief pitcher Chris Reitsma, so they released Dobbs. Gillick, who knew Dobbs from his time in Seattle, quickly snatched him up. Dobbs set the Phillies' all-time single-season record with 22 pinch-hits in 2008. He hit .301 with nine homers and 40 RBIs overall.

Pedro Feliz (signed as a free agent January 31, 2008). The Phillies signed Feliz because they thought he could add a little pop to their lineup and play solid defense. He had 14 homers, but he came up much bigger defensively. He had the second-best fielding percentage (.974) among NL third basemen. He made no errors in his final 33 games and just one error in his final 57 games. He knocked in the winning run in Game 5 of the World Series.

Ryan Howard (selected in the fifth round of the June 2001 draft). Howard fell to the fifth round in 2001 because, as assistant general manager Mike Arbuckle explained at the time, "He's a kid who we think had a case of draft-itis and didn't play as well as he's capable of playing this year. We took a little flier on him." Good move. He won NL Rookie of the Year in 2005, NL MVP in 2006, and led the majors with 48 homers and 146 RBIs in 2008. He hit .286 with three homers and six RBIs in the World Series.

Jimmy Rollins (selected in the second round of the June 1996 draft). Rollins had some of the best defensive tools of any high school player taken in the '96 draft, and those skills only improved. He eventually won Gold Gloves in 2007 and 2008. But Rollins could hit, too. He established himself as one of the best leadoff hitters in baseball before he won the NL MVP award in 2007. "God had that team draft me for a reason," Rollins said. "The door was open. There was only Kevin Sefcik at shortstop at the time, and that was it. It led to a speedy road. I always said from the beginning that I wanted to get to this organization and try to change the way people thought about it. I vowed I was going to try to change the face of this franchise, and along with a lot of other guys we were able to do that in 2008."

Chase Utley (selected 15th overall in the first round of the June 2000 draft). Most scouts agreed Utley was the best hitter in college baseball when the Phillies selected him, and he proved them right. He knocked in the first two runs in Game 1 of the NLDS against the Brewers. He hit a two-run homer in Game 1 of the World Series. He also threw out the go-ahead run on a play at the plate in the seventh inning in Game 5 of the World Series.

Utley capped the World Series celebration at Citizens Bank Park when he famously said, "World champions! World fucking champions!"

Outfielders

Pat Burrell (selected first overall in the first round of the June 1998 draft). A remarkable talent coming out of the University of Miami, Burrell's star rose quickly with the Phillies, but his most memorable moments might be his last two moments with the Phillies: 1) Hitting a leadoff double in the seventh inning in Game 5 of the World Series. It was his only hit of the World Series, and it led to pinch-runner Eric Bruntlett scoring the winning run. 2) Leading the championship parade down Broad Street.

Geoff Jenkins (signed as a free agent December 20, 2007). The Phillies lost Aaron Rowand to free agency after 2007, so they moved Shane Victorino to center field. But because they felt they needed help in right, they signed Jenkins thinking he could platoon with Jayson Werth. Werth ended up becoming an every-day player. But Jenkins, who had fallen into the background with just three at-bats the entire postseason, crushed a leadoff double in the sixth inning in Game 5 of the World Series. It led to a run in the 4–3 victory.

Matt Stairs (acquired from the Toronto Blue Jays on August 30, 2008, for Fabio Castro). The Phillies picked up Stairs because Jenkins was hurt at the time and they wanted another left-handed bat on the bench. He left his mark when he crushed a pinch-hit two-run home run to right field in the eighth inning to give the Phillies the lead in a 7–5 victory over the Los Angeles Dodgers in Game 4 of the NLCS.

So Taguchi (signed as a free agent December 23, 2007). The Phillies hoped he would be a pinch-hit extraordinaire, but it didn't work out that way. His biggest contribution came in an 8–6 victory over the Mets on July 22, when his two-run double in the ninth inning tied the game.

Shane Victorino (selected in Rule 5 draft on December 13, 2004). The Phillies took him in the Rule 5 draft, but he wasn't going to make the 25-man roster out of spring training 2005 so the

Phillies offered him back to the Dodgers. The Dodgers declined. Victorino joined Triple A Scranton/Wilkes-Barre and eventually established himself as an every-day player in the majors. He hit a grand slam off CC Sabathia in Game 2 of the NLDS. He had four RBIs in Game 2 of the NLCS. He hit a game-tying homer in Game 4 of the NLCS. He had a franchise record 13 RBIs in the postseason, breaking Lenny Dykstra's 11 RBIs in the 1993 postseason.

Jayson Werth (signed as a free agent December 18, 2006). The Dodgers didn't offer Werth a contract after the 2006 season because he had missed the entire season with a wrist injury. But Gillick knew him from his time in Baltimore and took a chance. Werth emerged as an everyday player in 2008. He not only set a career high with 24 homers, 67 RBIs, 73 runs scored, and 20 stolen bases, he hit .313 in the NLDS and .444 in the World Series.

GREAT PERFORMANCES

GOING THROUGH AN ART MUSEUM ON A MOTORCYCLE

The Phillies entered Game 5 of the 1980 National League Championship Series with more than just a World Series berth on the line.

They had fallen short in the NLCS in 1976, 1977, and 1978 and had finished fourth in the National League East in 1979. They had opportunities to win a championship but couldn't close. And because they couldn't close, their window of opportunity was just about shut.

They had to win Game 5 or they were finished.

"It was more or less told to us this was the last time they were going to keep us together if we didn't win this thing," Larry Bowa said.

The Phillies trailed the Houston Astros 5–2 in the eighth inning in the final game of the best-of-five series at the Astrodome, and Astros right-hander Nolan Ryan was his usual nasty self. But Bowa started the inning with a leadoff single, and Bob Boone chopped the next pitch back to the mound. The momentum from Ryan's delivery carried him away from the ball, and as he reached across his body to make the catch, the ball glanced off his glove and rolled away from him. Astros third baseman Enos Cabell fielded the ball and threw to first, but Boone had reached base safely. Pinch-hitter Greg Gross stepped into the batter's box. He was known for taking the first pitch, no matter what. Maybe that reputation relaxed Ryan. Maybe it caught the Astros flat-footed. Because Gross bunted Ryan's first pitch down the third-base line. Ryan got to the ball before Cabell, but by the time Ryan picked up the ball he didn't have a play at any base.

In a span of three pitches, the Phillies had the bases loaded with nobody out.

"I noticed that Enos Cabell was sort of talking to [Phillies third-base coach] Lee Elia at third," Gross said. "He was playing back. That's when I decided to bunt. I was notorious for taking a strike. If he's back and it's a strike, I'm going to try to bunt to load the bases with nobody out. If it's not a strike, it doesn't matter because they would come in. Only Nolan would know if he threw a pitch because he knew I was going to take so he could get ahead. That I don't know. I would never know that. But it would have to happen on the first pitch. The first pitch would have to be a strike. As it turned out, it worked out."

It was the first time Gross had bunted for a hit all year. The Phillies' dugout sprang to life as Pete Rose, who was 14-for-35 in his career against Ryan, strutted to the plate.

First pitch: fastball fouled back, 0–1.

Second pitch: fastball high, 1–1.

Third pitch: fastball high, 2–1.

Fourth pitch: fastball fouled back, 2–2.

Fifth pitch: breaking ball low, 3–2.

Sixth pitch: fastball fouled off Rose's leg, 3–2.

Seventh pitch: fastball outside, 4–2.

Ryan walked in a run to cut the Astros' lead to 5–3 with the bases still loaded and no outs. Astros manager Bill Virdon hopped out of the dugout to get Ryan and replace him with Joe Sambito. He got Keith Moreland, who pinch-hit for Bake McBride, to ground into a fielder's choice, which allowed Boone to score to make it 5–4. Ken Forsch entered to face Mike Schmidt and struck him out on a slider away.

Schmidt slapped at his bat as he returned to the dugout. No worries, Mike. Del Unser singled to right-center field on the first pitch to score Gross from third and make it 5–5.

"He jammed me with a fastball, and I got it over the second baseman's head," Unser said. "In that situation, you see it, you hit it."

Unser actually had an important pregame session with Phillies hitting coach Billy DeMars that he thought helped him immensely in that at-bat.

"Billy, let's go down and hit some," Unser said to DeMars before the game.

DeMars rolled his eyes.

"What the hell do you need?" he said.

"Something just isn't right," Unser said.

Unser was fine. He just had nervous energy.

"But anytime I had a session with Billy, I seemed to come out real good," Unser said.

Manny Trillo followed Unser with a triple to score Ramon Aviles, who pinch-ran for Moreland, and Unser to give the Phillies a 7–5 lead.

"The whole inning was crazy," Gross said. "Pete walked. There were chances for double plays. There were a lot of things going on in that inning, the same way there was the whole series. One time you're all excited because we've got a chance to go to the World Series. The next half-inning you're thinking we're going to be watching. It was that kind of thing. It was constant. The emotions were going up and down."

The Phillies lead wouldn't last. Tug McGraw gave up two runs in the bottom of the eighth inning to send the game into extra innings for the fourth time in the series.

"You're pacing," Gross said of the final innings. "But it seemed like things were going our way. You thought something good was going to happen."

Schmidt struck out to start the tenth, but Unser hit a smash over the head of Astros first baseman Dave Bergman into the right-field corner for a one-out double. Trillo flied out to center to move Unser to third with two outs. Garry Maddox stepped up with the biggest hit of his life when he hit a sinking line drive to center field. Center fielder Terry Puhl couldn't make the catch as Unser scored to make it 8–7.

Dick Ruthen, who replaced McGraw in the ninth, threw a perfect tenth inning to end the game and get the Phillies to their first World Series since 1950.

"There has never been a game like that one," McGraw said. "It was like going through an art museum on a motorcycle. You don't remember all the pictures you saw because there were too many and they came so fast."

HAPPY FATHER'S DAY

There is a specific two-step protocol for no-hitters and perfect games:

1. Keep your distance.
2. Keep your mouth shut.

Nobody is supposed to talk to a pitcher in the middle of a no-hitter or perfect game. Nobody. But what do you do when the pitcher throwing the no-hitter or perfect game breaks that rule?

Jim Bunning threw a no-hitter for the Detroit Tigers on July 20, 1958, against the Boston Red Sox on a steamy afternoon at Fenway Park. He had two outs in the bottom of the ninth inning when Ted Williams stepped into the batter's box. Williams was 39 years old and at the end of his Hall of Fame career. But he also was on his way to hitting .328 with 26 home runs and 85 RBIs. He could still hit.

Bunning got Williams to fly out to right field to end the game and preserve the no-hitter. His Tigers teammates mobbed him on the field before they carried the celebration into the visitors' clubhouse. Once inside the clubhouse, Bunning almost collapsed from exhaustion.

"It didn't hit me until afterward," he said. "I got in there, and I nearly fell over. I was drained, totally exhausted from the effort."

Flash forward to June 21, 1964.

Bunning, in his first season with the Phillies, stood on the mound on a hot Sunday afternoon at Shea Stadium against the New York Mets. It was Father's Day, which seemed fitting because Bunning was the father of seven children. Bunning had pitched

PHILLIES NO-NOS

Nine pitchers have thrown no-hitters in Phillies history. Jim Bunning has thrown the only perfect game.

Here are those nifty nine:

- August 29, 1885: Charles Ferguson vs. Providence, 1–0.
- July 8, 1898: Red Donahue vs. Boston, 5–0.
- September 18, 1903: Charles Fraser at Chicago, 10–0.
- May 1, 1906: Johnny Lush at Brooklyn, 6–0.
- June 21, 1964: Jim Bunning at New York, 6–0.
- June 23, 1971: Rick Wise at Cincinnati, 4–0.
- August 15, 1990: Terry Mulholland vs. San Francisco, 6–0.
- May 23, 1991: Tommy Greene at Montreal, 2–0.
- April 27, 2003: Kevin Millwood vs. San Francisco, 1–0.

splendidly for the Phillies to that point, going 6–2 with a 2.26 ERA. But he knew before the first inning that he had especially great stuff because he threw well in the bullpen. He felt even better after he threw a couple hanging sliders to Mets leadoff hitter Jim Hickman, who only could foul them off. Hickman struck out.

"If they aren't hitting those pitches, we could be in for one heck of a day," Bunning told catcher Gus Triandos.

The second, third, and fourth innings went without incident, but Jesse Gonder smashed a ball to Phillies second baseman Tony Taylor with one out in the fifth inning that became the game's greatest defensive play. Gonder hit the ball to Taylor's left, and Taylor knocked it down.

"It was the only change-up I had thrown in the whole game, and it convinced me not to throw another one," Bunning said.

The ball rolled a few feet away from Taylor, who quickly picked up the ball on the outfield grass. He threw to first base from his knees to get Gonder.

"When it hit my glove, I thought it might be a base hit," Taylor said. "But when I saw it stayed pretty close, I knew I could throw him out."

Bunning got Hawk Taylor to ground out to third baseman Richie Allen to end the fifth with the perfect game intact. Phillies manager Gene Mauch made some defensive changes before the bottom of the sixth. He had shortstop Cookie Rojas move to left field to replace Wes Covington. Bobby Wine took Rojas' place at shortstop.

It was about that time that Bunning started talking.

"Just nine more outs!"

"Dive!"

"Do something out there!"

"Come on! Let's get that perfect game!"

What in the hell was Bunning doing?

"In a game like that, the pressure not only builds on the pitcher but on the fielders as well," he said. "I was just trying to relieve it by talking."

It actually wasn't too out of character for Bunning. He always seemed to be talking during his starts.

"If he gave up a run he'd come into the dugout and say, 'OK, guys, that's it. That's all they're getting. Let's go. Let's get it back,'" Rojas said. "As far as the rest of the guys, they didn't want to jinx it, so they didn't say anything. He was talking. To the catcher, to the trainer, and all that stuff, back and forth. But as far as the players were concerned, they didn't say anything."

"He was silly on the mound whenever I went out to talk to him," Triandos said. "He was jabbering like a magpie. In the ninth inning, he told me to tell him a joke. I couldn't think of anything. All I could do was laugh."

Ron Hunt ripped a ball to third base with one out in the seventh, but Allen made the play. Bunning had two outs in the eighth when he ran a full count to Hawk Taylor. He needed a strike to keep the perfect game, and he got it with a slider.

"It was there," Bunning said.

"Caught the outside corner," Triandos said.

Bunning got Charley Smith to foul out to Wine on a 2–1 pitch. He got pinch-hitter George Altman to strike out swinging.

Bunning needed just one more out.

Mets manager Casey Stengel sent pinch-hitter Johnny Stephenson to the plate. Bunning liked his chances. He thought Stephenson had no chance to hit his curveball, so that's the only thing he threw. He worked the count to 2–2 on four consecutive curveballs.

Could the next pitch be a fastball?

Nope. Bunning stuck with his plan, threw Stephenson another curveball, and he swung and missed. Bunning pounded his fist into his glove. His teammates stormed the field. The 32,026 Mets fans in attendance cheered.

"I knew what I had done," Bunning said.

Perfection.

WE'RE GOING STREAKING!

If Jimmy Rollins and Chase Utley formed a comedy team, Rollins would play the funny man and Utley would play the straight man. Rollins is always smiling and laughing. Utley, well, he's not.

Their personalities showed in the ways they handled their historic hitting streaks in 2005 and 2006. Rollins had a 38-game hitting streak that ran from late 2005 through the first two games of 2006. He embraced every minute of it. Utley had a 35-game hitting streak in 2006, and he dodged questions like a presidential press secretary. Asked directly about his streak, Utley would come up with an answer totally unrelated.

"I thought we pitched really well today," he would say, setting up another cliche. "And pitching is the name of the game."

Rollins learned this about Utley, too. He mentioned the streak to Utley on July 21, 2006, after Utley extended his streak to 22 games with a single in his final at-bat in a victory over the Atlanta Braves at Citizens Bank Park. Utley barely uttered a response.

"You're superstitious?" Rollins said.

"Yeah," Utley replied.

"I just left him alone after that," Rollins said.

Rollins and Utley have two of the 10 longest hitting streaks in baseball history, which is impressive on its own. But they're also the first teammates in baseball history to have hitting streaks of 30 or more games.

Rollins started his streak slowly. He hit just .254 (15-for-59) with four doubles, one triple, and five RBIs through the first 13 games. Just two of those games were multi-hit games, so his streak, at least early on, didn't draw much attention. But then Rollins went off. He hit .451 (46-for-102) with 15 doubles, three triples, three home runs, and 17 RBIs in the final 23 games of the season to extend it to 36 games. He had 15 multi-hit games, including eight games with three hits. He then got hits in his first two games in 2006 to extend the hitting streak to 38 games, going 3-for-8 with three doubles before the streak ended April 6 against the St. Louis Cardinals at Citizens Bank Park.

Utley hit .405 (62-for-153) with 14 doubles, two triples, nine home runs, and 30 RBIs during his hitting streak. He had 23 multi-hit games, including four games with three hits.

"I think we both shared the same mentality," Utley said. "We weren't worried about getting a hit. We were worried about trying to help the team. Obviously, the more hits you get, the better chance your team has to win. But our whole goal is try to win that game. And [in 2005], the reason we had such a good run at the end was because Jimmy was always getting on base and scoring."

"Looking at his streak, every day it was two, three, or four hits," Rollins said. "It's like, 'This is stupid.' Two strikes, the pitcher would make a mistake and there's a double. I'm like, 'Is he serious?' But that's what it was like. It's like watching Ryan Howard hit home runs. Chase gets hits every day and it doesn't make any sense. You sit back and admire it. It's like, how much can he do?"

Rollins loved talking about his streak while it was happening. Utley would've preferred to talk about anything else.

"We're totally different types of people," Rollins said. "I try to work on his marketing. He doesn't want it."

"He's probably right," Utley said.

"I tell him all the time," Rollins said. "I told him during the

OPPOSITES ATTRACT

"Pressure? Well, it ain't hitting in 44 straight games, because I done that and it was fun." —Pete Rose

Pete Rose sees himself in Chase Utley.

Rose once said he would walk through hell in a gasoline suit to play baseball. Utley, who played with an injured hip throughout the 2008 season without complaint, is the same way. They play hard. They work hard.

"He comes to play every day, he works at being a good hitter, he studies pitchers, he gets his bat on the ball, he keeps himself in shape, he does all the things a great athlete should do. I admire him," Stan Musial said of Rose.

"Utley? I love that guy," George Brett said. "I love the way he plays. He plays hard and he plays right. When you do that, the numbers take care of themselves."

But while Rose and Utley share similar characteristics on the field, they couldn't be more different off the field. Rose had a 44-game hitting streak with the Reds in 1978, the third-longest streak in baseball history. Utley had a 35-game hitting streak with the Phillies in 2006, tied for the 10th-longest streak in history. Rose openly talked about his streak while it happened. Utley wouldn't say a word.

Rose couldn't understand that.

"What good is a hitting a streak...it's no good for baseball if you don't talk to the press," he said. "A hitting streak is for the country to follow. And they won't follow it if [you] say, 'I have no comment.'"

But that was Utley's way. He hates to talk about himself. He just wants to play, just like Rose. They just went about it in different ways.

streak, 'Just smile.' They already like him. They're already going to make him a superstar, so go ahead and be a superstar. Act like a superstar. Not mentally like, 'Oh, I'm a superstar.' You play hard. It's OK to smile."

"That's just the way I've always been," Utley said. "But I'm always having fun out there, smiling or not. The competition is fun. But he talks to me about smiling and marketing myself. He's working on me. But once you cross those lines...I try to stay even-keel, whether that's good or bad. That's the way I go about it."

It was tough for fans to stay on an even keel. Every time Rollins and Utley stepped to the plate during their streaks, they buzzed with anticipation.

"It's a pretty unique situation," Utley said. "The one thing I didn't want it to do [was] affect my approach at the plate. I didn't really want to change anything to try to get a hit. That's the last thing I wanted to do. There was support all the way until the last series in New York. That's how I felt. But I didn't put any extra pressure on myself. Either I was going to get a hit or I wasn't."

The streaks cemented the arrival of Rollins and Utley as two of the game's biggest stars.

"I want to be one of the greatest double-play combinations," Rollins said.

"We have something special," Utley said. "We're in a great city that loves baseball. And I think we're only going to get better."

FOR WHO? FOR WHAT?

Aaron Rowand turned around, dropped his head, and ran hard.

He *had* to make this catch.

Gavin Floyd had scuffled through his first seven starts in 2006. It always seemed like one bad inning killed him, and the first inning on May 11, 2006, against the New York Mets at Citizens Bank Park seemed to be that inning. Floyd had just walked the bases loaded with two outs, when Xavier Nady crushed a ball to deep center field. Rowand knew if he could catch the ball, maybe Floyd would settle and the Phillies could pick up an important victory against their National League East rival.

So Rowand ran. He took the perfect angle to the ball to give him a chance to make a play.

He remembered feeling the warning track underneath his feet as the ball landed in his glove. He remembered his face planting against the metal bar on the fence in center field. He remembered falling backward. He remembered holding onto the ball.

Aaron Rowand makes a leaping catch and crashes into the outfield wall during the game against the New York Mets at Citizens Bank Park in Philadelphia on May 11, 2006. The Phillies defeated the Mets 2–0.
Photo courtesy of AP Images.

"I just squeezed my glove until I stopped moving," Rowand said.

Rowand had made an incredible, full-speed, over-the-shoulder catch into the fence to save the game. He also broke his nose and suffered fractures around his left eye. Ken Griffey Jr. said the following day that the catch didn't impress him. What impressed him is that Rowand had the wherewithal to raise his glove to show the umpire he had the ball after suffering such a terrible impact.

"I've seen a lot of great catches," Charlie Manuel said. "To say that's the greatest catch…it becomes the greatest catch because of the effort and the determination and the want-to. I just think of the way he caught the ball. He had to know he was definitely going to hit the fence. I thought it was going out of the yard, but he kept running and you could tell he wasn't giving up on it."

Blood poured from the bridge of Rowand's nose and through both nostrils as he lay on the warning track. Catching instructor Mick Billmeyer quickly came from the bullpen with a towel.

"Squeeze my nose," Rowand said. "I can take it."

"I ain't squeezing your nose. You squeeze it," Billmeyer replied.

Billmeyer couldn't believe the amount of blood that Rowand had lost. It formed a puddle on the warning track.

"Usually it sinks, but it puddled up," Billmeyer said.

There have been more meaningful catches in Phillies history, but there hasn't been one more impressive because of the personal sacrifice involved. Fifty years from now when fans talk about the all-time greatest catches in Phillies history, it's tough to imagine Rowand's not being at the top of the list.

For who? For what?

Ricky Watters famously uttered those words when asked why he dropped a catchable ball for the Eagles.

Rowand had a much different answer.

"For who? My teammates. For what? To win," he responded.

Rowand weeks earlier had asked that the Phillies install padding on the fence to better protect himself. He saw the unprotected metal bars on the chain-link fence and sensed trouble. The padding arrived May 9, and the Phillies planned to install the padding while the team was away on a road trip that began May 12.

"They tried to get it as soon as they could," Rowand said. "You can't fault them. But I'm glad they put the padding on. I ran into it again later that year on the other side and bounced off it. I told

Mike [Burkholder, the Phillies' head groundskeeper] after the game, 'The padding works.'"

Rowand has seen the replay countless times. He hasn't tired of seeing it.

"I don't mind ever seeing good catches," he said. "I don't have to relive the pain of it, so it doesn't bother me very much."

LIGHTS-OUT LIDGE

The Phillies loved the scouting reports they had on Brad Lidge late in 2007.

"They said he was back," general manager Pat Gillick said.

Lidge had been one of the most dominant closers in baseball in 2004–05. But after a shaky '05 postseason with the Houston Astros, which included an infamous home run to Albert Pujols in the National League Championship Series against the St. Louis Cardinals, Lidge struggled. He had a 5.28 ERA in 2006, and he shuffled in and out of the closer's role in 2007.

The Phillies couldn't have cared less about those things because they knew what they saw, and they knew what it meant. *Lidge was back.* He still had his fastball, and his unhittable slider looked nastier than ever. Sure, Brett Myers had served them well as the team's closer in 2007, but if they could acquire Lidge they could return Myers to the rotation. It would be a 2-for-1 trade that would strengthen the rotation and bullpen.

Phillies assistant general manager Ruben Amaro Jr. started talking to Houston general manager Ed Wade, the former Phillies general manager who hired Amaro in Philadelphia. The talks started with relief pitcher Chad Qualls, but eventually turned to Lidge. Lidge had surgery on his right knee after the '07 season, but the Phillies were undeterred. They sent outfielder Michael Bourn, right-hander Geoff Geary, and minor-league third baseman Mike Costanzo to the Astros for Lidge and infielder Eric Bruntlett on November 7, 2007.

"It's tough to place a finger on it exactly, but I do feel that the last two years in Houston obviously have not been my best," Lidge said during his introductory news conference in Philadelphia. "I feel I'm capable of a lot better. So I hope and I really do believe the change of scenery will bring out the best in me."

Lidge reinjured the knee on the first pitch he threw to hitters in spring training, which caused some concern. The Phillies had acquired Freddy Garcia the previous offseason, but he proved to be one of the biggest busts in team history because a bad shoulder limited him to just one win. Phillies fans wondered if Lidge would be the next Garcia, but the Phillies weren't worried, even though Lidge required another surgery and started the season on the disabled list.

Lidge threw a scoreless inning in his Phillies debut April 6 in Cincinnati. He picked up his first save the next afternoon against the Reds. Lidge would go 41-for-41 in save opportunities in 2008 to become just the second pitcher in baseball to save at least 40 games in a season without blowing a save. Los Angeles Dodgers closer Eric Gagne, who went 55-for-55 in 2003, is the only other closer to accomplish the feat.

Lidge also went 7-for-7 in the postseason.

He capped his historic season by throwing the final pitch in Game 5 of the World Series to clinch the Phillies' first world championship since 1980.

"Oh my God. It was deafening," Lidge said. "I just had to make sure I took a deep breath. I took a step back because my heart was going 100 mph. It's indescribable. It had to be won here."

And people thought his best days were behind him.

"I can't believe how lucky I am," he said. "I can't believe how blessed I am to be on this team. I'm thanking God for being right here, right now, for this year, for everyone around me. You go through a lot to be in this position. I wouldn't change anything in my career because it all got me right here, right now. This is the best it could ever be."

Off the Field

THE PHANATIC

Philadelphia has an affinity for Ben Franklin, in case the thousands of Ben Franklin statues, sculptures, murals, and other artwork scattered across the city haven't given it away.

Franklin had been a one-man show for years until he started to share his iconic status in Philadelphia in 1978, when the Phillies introduced the Phillie Phanatic at Veterans Stadium. Before the Phanatic's introduction, the Phillies had employed Colonial mascots Phil and Phyllis, who stood on the field in their rigid costumes and waved at people.

Boring.

So when former Phillies director of marketing Dennis Lehman took a West Coast road trip with the team in 1977 and saw how the San Diego Chicken energized and entertained the crowd at Jack Murphy Stadium, he thought a mascot could have a similar effect on Phillies fans. Lehman and Phillies promotion director Frank Sullivan pitched the idea to develop a new mascot to Phillies executive vice president Bill Giles, who told the pair to go for it. They contacted Jim Henson, who created the Muppets. Henson wasn't interested but referred them to Bonnie Erickson and Wayde Harrison, who ran a design studio in Brooklyn. Erickson had designed Miss Piggy and Statler and Waldorf, the wise-cracking geezers that sat in the balcony on *The Muppet Show*.

Giles said he asked them to make the mascot fat, green, indistinguishable, and loveable.

"I kind of wanted him cuddly, something little kids would like to hug," Giles said. "I really don't know why I said green."

The Phillies reviewed several sketches from Erickson and Harrison. Giles liked them, but he wanted something more. He wanted the Phanatic fatter. He wanted his nose bigger. He got it, although even then he wasn't convinced it would work.

"I was kind of hiding when he first came out," Giles said. "I thought it was going to be a bomb."

Giles' skepticism was evident. He said Erickson and Harrison offered him two prices for the Phanatic design: $2,900 without the copyright and $5,000 with the copyright. Giles, not believing a big, fat, green mascot would work in Major League Baseball, thought he might as well save the team the extra $2,100 and bought the Phanatic without the copyright.

The Phillies eventually paid more than $200,000 for it.

The Phanatic was a hit.

"We sent along a personality sketch for the Phanatic," Harrison said, "but we didn't get too specific. You want the performer to fill in the blanks and give him an opportunity to create the character."

That performer was Dave Raymond, who was a 21-year-old intern in the promotions department.

"I didn't know what to expect, and neither did anyone else," Raymond said. "They just told me to do what I wanted to do and have fun. I quickly realized the character had a life and an energy of its own. I was really sick one Opening Day, but as soon as I put the costume on, I felt fine. Then, I'd take a break and I felt horrible. Put the costume back on and felt fine. I went in the hospital the next day with pneumonia and a 104-degree fever."

The Phanatic mimicked Phillies batting stances during pregame introductions. He danced with ladies on top of the dugout. He stuck out his party-favor tongue at the opposition and grabbed hold of his belly to make people laugh. He smashed plastic Mets helmets and streaked across the field.

Kids and adults loved him.

Raymond played the Phanatic through 1993, when Tom Burgoyne took over. He has been the Phanatic ever since.

"The Phanatic has become more than just a Phillies guy," Giles said. "Most of the Philadelphia marketing for the city includes a picture of him. He's become a bit of an icon in the city."

Some might say Chase Utley, Ryan Howard, or Jimmy Rollins are the face of the Phillies, but in truth it is the Phanatic. Ask a non-baseball fan what they think of when they think of the Phillies, and they are almost certain to say that fat green mascot.

STILL AN ORIGINAL

Dave Raymond was the man inside the Phanatic costume from 1978 to 1993.

He has fought with Tommy Lasorda (literally), got the cold shoulder from Deion Sanders (it was just an act), and made the Phanatic the institution it is today. He considers his greatest moments as the Phanatic the World Series championship parade in 1980 and sitting in the dugout in the Astrodome in Houston when the Phillies clinched the National League pennant in 1980.

"When we won that game, they had the champagne in the locker room and it all breaks out," Raymond said. "I guess I was 20, 21, and drank the champagne. I got completely blitzed in about 40 minutes. Greg Luzinski sees that I'm blitzed and says, 'Hey, kid, you're not supposed to drink this [stuff]. You're supposed to spray it on people.'"

He learned his lesson. Raymond, who is Emperor of Fun and Games for the Raymond Entertainment Group, recalled some of his other memorable moments as the Phanatic:

Moment he'd like to forget?

"All the bumps, bruises, and heat. But one that comes to mind that was the scariest was back in the day when people could smoke in the stands. I would take my three-wheeler in the stands. I could pop wheelies pretty quickly without a lot of speed or energy. In this particular case, I popped a wheelie and the gas cap actually leaked and spilled gasoline on me. And this one fan is ready to flick his cigarette down. He didn't notice what was going on. I went, 'Oh my God. I've got gas in the crotch of a furry, green Muppet and this guy is going to flick his cigarette and I'm going to explode.' The only thing that crossed my mind was, 'Well, they'll never forget me.' Fortunately for me it didn't happen."

Favorite sketch or bit?

"One day Bill Giles said go out with the grounds crew when they change bases in the fifth inning. I accidentally knocked over one of the grounds-crew guys and everybody laughed. So from that developed a routine I called the *Gong Show* routine. Chuck Barris would be doing his thing, and all of a sudden Gene Gene the Dancing Machine would come out. He would walk out on stage and this song would play. And Gene would just do this little move. People went nuts. [Phillies organist] Paul Richardson would play that song. I would run around the bases, knock over the grounds crew, we would all come together and dance to 'Gene Gene the Dancing Machine.' We'd get 25,000 to 30,000 standing ovations. That led us to believe that Phillies fans were either starved for entertainment or we were actually good. But it was the fact that they never saw a character and the grounds crew on a major-league team start dancing. That really was the genesis of all these minor-league grounds crews. Now you see them dancing. I believe that was created by the Phanatic and the Phillies grounds crew."

Bit that bombed?

"We did a routine on the dugout where we put a midget in a trunk and I opened the trunk and the midget jumped out and started playing the saxophone. We got one of those claps where like 12 people clapped. You could see people looking around saying, 'What the hell was that?' So we threw the midget back in the trunk and ran off to the dugout. It was not accepted very well."

What do you remember about interacting with the players, coaches, and managers?

"The players before the game just gravitated to the Phanatic to play tricks on him or vice versa. That all started because of players like Willie Stargell. I realized, 'Hey, the players actually will let me fool around with them pregame.' It was just the acceptance of the players that the Phanatic would be fun. He didn't necessarily

The Philadelphia Phillies' mascot, Phillie Phanatic, watches the umpire dust off home plate.

make you look bad unless you wanted him to. Players started coming to me and saying so-and-so last night, blah, blah, blah. It was stuff that wasn't family entertainment. So when they introduced that player I would do something nonverbally that reminded that particular player that I knew what happened—just for the benefit of the other players on the bench and that player looking at me going, 'How does he know that?' Fans would think I was just mimicking some of the players. The players were telling me stuff that nobody else knew. The guy didn't wake up on time and missed the bus, so I would make it look like I was oversleeping. Or Sid Bream from the Pirates. They used to call him the Beached Whale because he was so slow. And so when they introduced Sid Bream I would fall down and flop around like a beached whale. He would be giving me the finger, and all the other players would be laughing."

And that led to the fight with Tommy Lasorda?

"Steve Sax would get me his jersey all the time. When Tommy was telling the clubbie, 'Don't give the Phanatic my jersey,' Steve Sax would steal it and say, 'Don't tell I gave it to you,' because they loved to see Tommy get pissed. They would all be laughing and Tommy would be yelling obscenities. And that led up to the fight. I thought Tommy was playing along. I didn't know he actually was getting more mad and more upset. And then he finally came out and tackled me and started to beat me up."

Favorite player to impersonate?

"I loved doing Tommy because he was short, fat, and pigeon-toed. But guys like Dave Parker, who acted like he was mad. Deion Sanders. I dressed a dummy in a purple fedora with jewelry. I did it and thought he was mad. The next day I get a knock on the door. I opened the door and it's Deion Sanders, and I said, 'Uh-oh, he's going to punch me in the nose.' He said, 'Oh, man, listen, the last time I was in town you did the thing with the dummy dressed up like me. My family and friends are here, can you do that today?' So I did it. He's there in the dugout and he never cracked a smile. He looked at me like he was going to kill me. He didn't want anybody else to know he really liked it, but he wanted to see his family see it."

Something fans might not know about the Phanatic?

"Yeah, when they first delivered the costume they said there would be no way to clean it. For the first year of its existence it never got cleaned, and it smelled horribly. Then what I did out of pure frustration, I said, 'This is crazy.' I took the costume home, put it in the bathtub, filled up the tub with some water and detergent, and it came out fine. It smelled better. I went to the people who created it in New York, and they said, 'You can wash these things.' Oh, great, good news."

MR. BASEBALL

The Phillies have entertained since 1883. It just depends on the definition of entertainment.

Few have entertained better and longer than Bob Uecker. He appeared on *The Tonight Show* with Johnny Carson 13 times. He hosted *Saturday Night Live* for an episode in 1984. He starred in the TV show *Mr. Belvedere* from 1985 to 1990. He starred in countless Miller Lite commercials. He made "Juuuuuuuuuust a bit outside" a movie quote favorite from *Major League*, where he stole the show as Cleveland Indians broadcaster Harry Doyle.

Uecker played for the Phillies in 1966 and part of 1967, after the St. Louis Cardinals traded Dick Groat, Bill White, and Uecker to Philadelphia on October 25, 1965, for Art Mahaffey, Pat Corrales, and Alex Johnson.

"Of course, I was the main player in the deal," Uecker said. "I didn't want to go, but I thought, *Well, if I don't go it's going to be the end for Dick Groat and Bill White.* So that was the only reason I agreed to go to Philadelphia."

Groat was a five-time All-Star. He won the National League MVP for the Pittsburgh Pirates in 1960. White was also a five-time All-Star. He had finished third in the NL MVP voting in 1964. Uecker? He had hit a combined .224 with four home runs and 24 RBIs in parts of four seasons with the Milwaukee Braves and Cardinals before he put on a Phillies uniform. Uecker, who was a catcher, hit .208 in 1966 with the Phillies. He set career highs in at-bats (207), hits (43), home runs (7), and RBIs (30).

"And then I started realizing what I was doing and I said, 'Man, I've got to lay back or they're going to expect this every year,'" Uecker said. "So I kind of backed off. I thought to myself, *What are you going to do after you're done playing if you keep hitting like this? You won't have anything to talk about. No stories. No jokes.* So I'd go up there and try to make an out sometimes."

He did. He hit .171 in 18 games for the Phillies in 1967, and they traded him to the Atlanta Braves on June 6 for Gene Oliver. Uecker, who lived with teammates in an apartment complex on City Line Avenue in Philadelphia, enjoyed his time with the Phillies. He became close friends with Dick Allen, whom Uecker calls one of his favorite people of all time.

"Richie was into horses. He loved horses. Still does," Uecker said. "He told me that he was going to bring his horse down to the Presidential Apartments on a day off. I don't know how he did it, but he did. He rode that horse down there somehow. He went through yards and everything else, but he got that horse down there to the Presidential Apartments. I went outside, and there he was, sitting on that horse. It was great. We used to sit in the back of the plane and harmonize, sing songs, me and Richie. We could sing, yeah. We were good. We'd sing those barbershop songs and harmonize. Nothing *American Idol*, but some kind of idol. Buddah idol."

Uecker got a chance to learn the game from Gene Mauch. He got to experience Philadelphia fans, too.

"The fans there are totally fanatic about baseball," Uecker said. "The only fight I ever had with a fan was in Philadelphia. The Philly fans get a little tough sometimes. This particular fan was on me for about four nights in a row. I don't know why I was playing four nights in a row in the first place, but I was in the on-deck circle, and they were really on me, so I dove into the seats and started throwing punches and everything. I was happy I got it out of the way. The only problem with that was a lawsuit. I can remember walking into the courtroom, and she was sitting there with her attorney and still pretty well marked up. Which means I beat up a woman."

On June 17, 1966, the Phillies were playing in St. Louis. It was the top of the third inning and the Phillies were leading 3–2 with

The Phillie Phanatic dances on a float in front of City Hall during the World Championship Parade October 31, 2008, in Philadelphia. The Phillies defeated the Tampa Bay Rays to win their first World Series in 28 years.

the bases loaded and two outs. The Cardinals had just replaced left-hander Curt Simmons for Mahaffey, who threw right-handed. Uecker, who was hitting .257 at the time, had flied out to left field in his first at-bat in the second. But he had a chance here to break the game wide open.

Mauch pulled him for Clay Dalrymple.

Yes, Uecker got pinch-hit for in the third inning.

It kind of made sense. Dalrymple hit left-handed. Mahaffey threw right-handed. Uecker didn't exactly have the greatest track record in the world.

"Art Mahaffey threw a wild pitch and a run scored," Uecker said. "And Gene winked at me like he made a genius move. Like I couldn't take a wild pitch? Geez, we're all trained to do that. But he did. He pinch-hit Clay Dalrymple for me, and when Art Mahaffey threw a wild pitch he looked at me and winked, like, 'Was that a move or what?' What could I say? It worked. Nice going."

Uecker said playing for Mauch was one of his greatest thrills in baseball. Mauch was old school and Uecker liked that.

"He'd come up to you when you were on the bench and say, 'What are you doing here?'" Uecker said. "Uh, watching the game. 'Get out in the bullpen.' OK, I went to the bullpen. He'd call out there, 'What the hell are you doing out there?' Uh, I don't know. I'm not in the game. 'Get back here.' I loved Gene. I really did. He'd walk by in the dugout and all of a sudden he'd jump up on you, 'What's the count? What's the score?' To make sure you were in the game. Man, he was great. Gene was three or four innings ahead of where you were in the game, all of the time. He really was."

Mauch and the Phillies provided Uecker some great memories and a lifetime's worth of material.

HEY, HOW YA DOIN'?

"Hello, Pete. This is Ronald Reagan."

"How ya doing?"

Pete Rose became the National League's all-time hits leader August 10, 1981, when he slapped a single through the hole into left field at Veterans Stadium. It was the 3,631st hit of his career.

It was a remarkable moment in front of 60,561 fans, but it was the show afterward that many people remember as much as (or maybe even more than) the hit. In the bowels of Veterans Stadium, a throng of reporters had gathered for Rose's postgame news conference. He already had gotten a handshake from Commissioner

Bowie Kuhn. He had received congratulations from teammates, coaches, and Phillies owners and executives. But he had one more congratulations to get, and that was coming from President Ronald Reagan.

A red phone—apparently only Batman and presidents make calls on red phones—sat next to Rose as he chatted up reporters.

The phone rang.

"Tell the president wait a minute," Rose joked.

Rose picked up.

"One moment please."

Rose waited, waited, and waited.

"Maybe the operators have gone on strike?" he said.

The wait continued.

"Good thing there isn't a missile on the way."

Disconnected. The phone rang two more times before Reagan could be heard on the other end. Reagan said hello, which was when Rose memorably answered, "How ya doing?" to the most powerful man in the world.

"What the fuck am I supposed to say?" Rose said. "That's the way I answer the phone."

And that's why Rose endeared himself to so many people when he played. He was real, and he kept it real regardless of the person, place, or situation.

"I'll tell you," Reagan said. "I've had as much trouble getting this line. I think I had to wait longer than you did to break the record."

"We were gonna give you five more minutes and that was it," Rose responded.

"I just wanted to call and congratulate you," Reagan said. "I know how you must feel, and I think it's great."

"Well, thank you very much," Rose said. "I know you're a baseball fan, and we appreciate your taking time out to call us here in Philadelphia. I know all the fans appreciate it, and Pete Rose and Pete Rose II appreciate it, too."

"I can tell you that you are right about being a fan," Reagan said. "And as a matter of fact, I was a sports announcer broadcasting Major League Baseball before I ever had any kind of a job like

I have now. But this is really a thrill, and I know how everyone must feel about it after the long dry spell waiting for the season to get under way [following a 50-day midseason strike], and you've really brought it in style."

"Well, thank you very much," Rose said. "You play a good football player, too."

They exchanged their good-byes and Rose hung up the phone. He continued his news conference from there. But that entire conversation encapsulated Rose perfectly. No pretenses. No nothing. It was a famous baseball player talking to the most powerful man on the planet, but Rose talked to Reagan like he was a Phillies fan he had bumped into outside the ballpark.

"You've got to remember I've got a couple hundred guys down there at a press conference," Rose said. "And the phone rings three different times. I'm there because I just set the National League record for hits. And every time I picked up the phone, the guy says, 'Hold on for the president.' And then he'd hang up. And finally on the third call, he says, 'Hello, Pete, this is the president.' I said, 'Hey, how ya doin'?'"

"Here's the deal, this is the way I am. I have all the respect in the world for the President of the United States or a senator or whomever. But I'm the type of guy that—I don't talk down to anybody. I don't talk up to anybody, either. I talk to the person. I've been in front of Gerald Ford and Richard Nixon. I met Dwight Eisenhower, Jimmy Carter, and Ronald Reagan. He's a great guy and everything, but I'm in the midst of this press conference, talking about how it feels to break one of the great players in baseball history's records—Stan Musial's hit record—this phone keeps ringing and bothering me. That was my philosophy on that. I didn't mean anything disrespectful to the president, and I don't think he understood that. I don't understand why everybody got such a kick out of that. If you say, 'Hey, Pete,' I'm going to say, 'How ya doin'?' What am I supposed to say? I picked up the phone three times already and there was nobody on there. Jeffrey Dahmer is on there as far as I'm concerned."

MAKING THEIR MARK

Jimmy Rollins quietly packed his bags and cleaned out his locker after Game 6 of the 2009 World Series.

He had just watched the New York Yankees celebrate their 27th World Series championship at Yankee Stadium, ending the Phillies' dreams of becoming the first National League team to win consecutive World Series since the 1975–76 Cincinnati Reds. The Reds were known as the Big Red Machine, and Rollins had hoped the Phillies could make a name for themselves, too.

"Maybe they'll call us the Little Red Machine," he said.

But the Yankees ended those aspirations with a 7–3 victory in Game 6.

"You won't get to wear Harry's jacket now," a reporter mentioned to Rollins as he grabbed items from his locker.

"I know," he said. "It's going back to his family now."

Rollins had celebrated the Phillies' third consecutive NL East championship at Citizens Bank Park on September 30, and his thoughts turned to Kalas, the beloved Phillies broadcaster who died April 13. Kalas had called Phillies games since 1971 and had called the unforgettable final out of the 2008 World Series. The 2009 season had not been the same without Kalas, whose memorable powder-blue sport coat and white loafers were placed in the Phillies dugout before every game during the season as a memorial.

"We get to Broad Street again, you'll see HK's jacket and shoes on my back and feet," Rollins said that night. "There is no doubt about it. When we're going down Broad Street, if it happens again, believe me, I will be rocking it."

It would take a lot of things to go right for that to happen.

It took a lot of things to go right just to get to this point.

Just two teams had won consecutive World Series since the Big Red Machine: the 1992–93 Toronto Blue Jays and the 1998–2000 Yankees. The odds were against a repeat, but the Phillies were motivated to beat the odds.

"That's the only way you can be remembered as being great," Rollins said after the Phillies clinched the NL pennant on October 21. "You want to have people remember your team, and individuals that were on that team when you look back. You can say, 'You know what? That team was pretty good.' Everybody knows about the Yankees. Everybody knows about Boston and all the great players. Obviously, we want that here. When people refer to Philadelphia, not just as a team that was first to lose 10,000 games, but a team that was able to play with the best at their time."

How far the Phillies had come. They were thrilled to win the NL East in 2007, partially because it meant they no longer had to hear about the 1993 team, the last Phillies team to make the play-offs. And they knew when they won the 2008 World Series they no longer had to be constantly reminded of the 1980 team.

These Phillies already had made their mark in Philadelphia. They had changed the culture of a franchise and a city.

"I was in a unique situation coming here to really see a transformation on both ends—not only the organization, but the fans and the city," right fielder Jayson Werth said. "I feel like I was here for the old Philly and the old Phillies, and I'm here for the new Philly and the new Phillies."

The new Phillies wanted to go even bigger, but they found going bigger would be difficult. Brad Lidge went from being the best relief pitcher in baseball in 2008 to the worst. Cole Hamels struggled like he had never struggled before. Rollins hit just .205 through July 1. J.C. Romero missed the beginning of the season with a 50-game suspension for violating baseball's policy against performance-enhancing substances and missed most of the

Chase Utley hits a solo home run off New York Yankees relief pitcher Phil Coke as New York Yankees catcher Jorge Posada looks on in the seventh inning of Game 5 of the 2009 World Series on November 2, 2009, in Philadelphia. Photo courtesy of AP Images.

second half of the season with an injured elbow that required surgery. Brett Myers missed much of the season after surgery on his right hip. The bench struggled. The bullpen struggled. The rotation struggled until general manager Ruben Amaro Jr. found reinforcements in July.

"Everyone was gunning for us," Rollins said. "The last couple years we were kind of the dark horse. We were right there, but we were never in the lead. We were trailing and catching up at the end. But winning a championship, everyone is gunning for us."

But it also showed how much talent the Phillies had that they could play an entire season with targets on their backs, injuries, and bad years and still cruise to the division title. The Phillies moved into first place in the NL East on May 30 and remained there the rest of the year. Of course, it helped to have a lineup with five All-Stars: center fielder Shane Victorino, second baseman Chase Utley, first baseman Ryan Howard, Werth, and Ibanez. The Phillies led the league in scoring with 820 runs. They were the only team in the National League to have 200 or more home runs and 100 or more stolen bases. Howard (45), Werth (36), Ibanez (34), and Utley (31) became the 12th foursome in baseball history to have 30 or more home runs in a season.

The arrivals of Cliff Lee and Pedro Martinez helped. Lee, who the Phillies acquired in a July 29 trade with the Cleveland Indians, went 7–4 with a 3.39 ERA in 12 regular-season starts. Martinez, who the Phillies signed to a one-year contract July 15, went 5–1 with a 3.63 ERA in nine starts. The Phillies had a 4.61 ERA at the All-Star break, which ranked 25th in baseball, but had a 3.65 ERA after the break, which ranked fifth.

They won the division by six games.

Lee threw a complete-game 5–1 victory against the Colorado Rockies in Game 1 of the NL Division Series. The Phillies lost Game 2 but won Game 3 6–5 at Coors Field. Game 3 had to be postponed a day because of snow and cold, but the 35-degree game-time temperature still matched the lowest temperature for a playoff game. Rollins got a leadoff single in the top of the ninth inning against Rockies closer Huston Street and scored on a sacrifice fly from Howard to win it.

The Phillies won Game 4 5–4 to clinch a NL Championship Series rematch against the Los Angeles Dodgers. The Phillies blew a one-run lead in the eighth as the Rockies scored three runs to make it 4–2. But Rollins got things started again with a one-out single against Street. Utley worked a two-out walk, and Howard doubled to right field to clear the bases to tie the game. Werth followed with a single to right to score Howard to win it.

"We really believe that we can do it," said Lidge, who picked up the save. "We know that if we do we can form—I don't want to say a legacy—but some kind of pretty cool thing in this game. It's too early to say legacy, but I think we've got a lot of swagger on this team. The guys just don't want to be known as one-time

World Series winners. They want to be in the same sentence as some of the great teams."

They needed just five games to beat the Dodgers in the NLCS. Ibanez's three-run home run to right field in the eighth helped them win Game 1 8–6 at Dodger Stadium. They returned to Philadelphia with the Series tied but watched Lee throw eight shutout innings in a 3–0 victory in Game 3.

Game 4 provided dramatics similar to Game 4 of the NLDS against the Rockies and Game 4 of the 2008 NLCS against the Dodgers. The Phillies trailed 4–3 in the ninth, when Dodgers closer Jonathan Broxton walked Matt Stairs on four pitches with one out. Broxton promptly drilled Carlos Ruiz with his next pitch to put runners on first and second. Greg Dobbs softly lined out for the second out, which put the game in the hands of Rollins.

Rollins came through again. He ripped a double to right-center field to clear the bases and win the game. The Phillies pummeled the Dodgers 10–4 in Game 5 to clinch their second consecutive trip to the World Series.

But the Yankees proved to be too much. Lee pitched brilliantly in a complete-game 6–1 victory in Game 1, but old problems resurfaced. Hamels could not hold a 3–0 lead in an 8–5 loss in Game 3 at the Bank. Pedro Feliz hit a clutch game-tying home run in the eighth inning in Game 4, but Lidge blew the game in the ninth. Johnny Damon hit a two-out single in a nine-pitch at-bat to get things started. He stole second and third on the same play because the Phillies had nobody covering third on a defensive shift for Mark Teixeira. It led to three runs and a 7–4 loss.

Lee sent the series back to New York with a victory in Game 5, but the Yankees battered Martinez in Game 6.

The Phillies would not repeat, but they left the clubhouse that night believing this wasn't the end.

"It will be interesting to see five, 10 years from now what we were able to accomplish," Lidge said. "Not just this year but hopefully next year and the year after. Hopefully we did some pretty amazing things. But with the players we have here...I think we have the opportunity to do something pretty special."

They already had. Since Manuel arrived in 2005, the Phillies had the best record in the National League at 447–363. They had won their second World Series in franchise history. They had played in consecutive World Series for the first time and had played in the postseason three consecutive years for the second time.

It could be argued that this was the Golden Age of Phillies baseball.

"Looking into the future, I don't really see anything changing," Rollins said.

CHARLIE

The party continued in the Phillies clubhouse, where players soaked themselves in beer and champagne, and on the field, where 45,000 fans sang and cheered and rocked Citizens Bank Park.

Charlie Manuel celebrated, but in the quiet of his office.

"Champagne gets in my eyes," he said from the chair behind his desk. "It burns my damn eyes. I got some VO up here, though."

Manuel did not need to satisfy his ego the night the Phillies won the 2008 World Series. He did not need to be in the middle of the action, taking credit for what had just happened. He managed the Phillies because he loved baseball and because he loved to win. He said as much November 4, 2004, when the Phillies introduced him as their new manager.

"I'm a baseball guy," he said. "I hear guys say, 'Well, he's a lifer.' I'm not a lifer. You know what I am? I'm a 24-hour-a-day baseball guy. I live and sleep baseball."

His words held true October 29, 2008, when the Phillies won it all. Manuel did not seek attention that night. The Phillies won, and that was good enough for him. Let the players have their moment while he relaxed in his office.

"What's up, Harry?" Manuel said as Phillies broadcaster Harry Kalas entered the room.

Phillies manager Charlie Manuel (right) talks with former manager Dallas Green on the first day of the team's spring training for pitchers and catchers in Clearwater, Florida, on February 14, 2008. Photo courtesy of AP Images.

"Charlie!" Kalas said with a big smile on his face. "Nice going! Nice job! Nice going!"

"How about the Fightins?!" Manuel said.

Kalas offered his thanks and left. Manuel turned back to the people who had gathered, including Dallas Green, who managed the Phillies to their first World Series championship in 1980. "This is better than I imagined," Manuel said. "It's better when you see the people that are happy and the people that enjoy it. It's good for everybody. It's good for the city, our fans, the organization, all of our players. It wasn't easy. It definitely wasn't easy. But it was worth it."

Somebody mentioned to Manuel that he and Green are the only two managers in Phillies history to win championships.

"That's good," Manuel said. "One of these days I might get a job like Dallas."

"Hopefully you don't have to wait 28 years to get it," Green replied.

Manuel laughed.

"People think this is a piece of cake," said Green, who has been a senior advisor to the general manager since 1998. "And the thing is, Charlie had to go through an extra playoff. I only went through one playoff. He went through two playoffs to get to the World Series."

"It's hard to win, period," Manuel added. "It's hard to win, isn't it? It's hard to win. You've got to have the talent, but some fight comes into play."

"I love these guys," Green continued. "These guys have proven to me that they're a hell of a baseball team. They care about winning. They care about playing the game. I've told anybody who will listen that they're a resilient team. They always were. They come to play every day. And Charlie has them convinced that you don't get too high and you don't get too low and you just play the game. He did it differently than I would have, but that's what managing is all about."

And what did Green think of the way he did it?

"What the hell? He's going to have a ring on," Green said. "Everybody bitched and moaned about how I did it, but I've got a ring. They can bitch all they want about him, but he's going to have a ring. And we're the only two guys in 126 years that have a ring. I welcome him with open arms because that seat is a tough seat in Philadelphia. Everybody knows that. It's a tough seat anywhere, but in Philadelphia it's a tough seat. And he has gone through some very difficult times with you guys, the fans and everybody. But he has weathered the storm, and he has proven to everybody that he is a pretty damn good baseball man. And that's what it takes to be a champion."

NOTES

CHAPTER 1 - THE GOOD

The Longest Outs
"If I don't get out of this inning...": McGraw, Tug, *Ya Gotta Believe!* (New York: New American Library, 2004), p. 149.

Still Crazy After All These Years
"All the people who called us rejects...": Fitzpatrick, Frank, "Bring on Blue Jays!" *The Philadelphia Inquirer*, October 14, 1993, section Sports, D1.

"We went out and added more gypsies, tramps and thieves...": Hagen, Paul, "The Wild Bunch," *Philadelphia Daily News*, April 5, 1993, section Sports, B6.

The Whiz Kids
"My wrist was bothering me...": Didinger, Ray, "Sisler Saves Whiz Kids," *Philadelphia Daily News*, Sept. 25, 1986, section Sports, G32.

The Wheeze Kids
"We feel the team is not performing as well as we anticipated...": Pascarelli, Peter, "Corrales is fired by the Phillies," *The Philadelphia Inquirer*, section Sports, A1.

"Somehow it seems fitting...": Boswell, Thomas, "Mea Culpa Isn't Part of Phillies," *The Washington Post*, July 20, 1983, section Sports, D1.

"It was tough to let Pat go...": Fitzpatrick, Frank, "A summer of grumbling, loose lips and palace intrigue," *The Philadelphia Inquirer*, July 17, 2003, section Sports, E2.

First and Forgotten

"I don't blame Charlie for everything that happened last year...": Westcott, Rich, *Phillies Essential* (Chicago: Triumph Books, 2006), p. 28-33.

"Moran was an inspiring leader...": Westcott, Rich and Bilovsky, Frank, *The Phillies Encyclopedia* (Philadelphia: Temple University Press, 2004), p. 331-332.

CHAPTER 2 – THE BAD

Black Friday

"It was a packed house...": Carchidi, Sam, "'77 Phils were riding high ... then came the nightmare," *The Philadelphia Inquirer*, May 15, 2003, section Sports, D2.

"I can still see the play...": Smith, Claire, "Ump's fingerprints were on Phils' Black Friday playoff mess," *The Philadelphia Inquirer*, July 18, 2006, section Sports, E5.

No! No! No! No! No!

"If I'd had a gun, I would have shot him...": Fitzpatrick, Frank, "Oh, why did Chico go?" *The Philadelphia Inquirer*, Sept. 21, 1989, section Sports, C1.

"It was like Ted Williams hitting..." Hochman, Stan, "The Survivors of '64," Philadelphia Daily News, section Sports, p. 86.

CHAPTER 3 – THE UGLY

The Dark Ages

"The Phillies sold the office furniture one year...": Westcott, Rich, *Phillies Essential* (Chicago: Triumph Books, 2006), p. 45-49.

"Sometimes there were so few fans at the park...": Westcott, Rich, *Philadelphia's Old Ballparks* (Philadelphia: Temple University Press, 1996), p. 58.

"Nugent makes pennants in Philadelphia...": Westcott, Rich and Bilovsky, Frank, *The Phillies Encyclopedia* (Philadelphia: Temple University Press, 2004), p. 371-373.

A Decade After Jackie

"Bring that nigger here with the rest of your team...": Kram, Mark, "The Nightmare that was Philly," Philadelphia Daily News, April 9, 1997, section Sports, p. 10.

Baker Bowl

"Home runs have become too cheap at the Philadelphia ball park...": Westcott, Rich, *Philadelphia's Old Ballparks* (Philadelphia: Temple University Press, 1996), p. 27-98.

CHAPTER 4 - IN THE CLUTCH
Break on Through

"I wanted a stance that gave me a strike zone like Pete Rose's...": Schmidt, Mike and Walder, Barbara, *Always on the Offense* (New York: Athenewn, 1982), p. 55-57.

"You've got Pete Rose, who exemplifies what a captain out to be...": Hochman, Stan, *Mike Schmidt: Baseball's King of Swing* (New York: Random House, 1983), p. 84.

"The last few weeks of the regular season as well as the World Series...": Kashatus, William C., "Pride of the Philadelphia Phillies: An Interview with Mike Schmidt," *Pennsylvania Heritage*, Fall 1995, p. 17.

"Sometimes you'll hear one player saying about another...": Schmidt, Mike and Walder, Barbara, *Always on the Offense* (New York: Athenewn, 1982), p. 177.

"Pete instilled in me a new vitality...": Dolson, Frank, "MVP Mike: Schmidt Flattered at Unanimous Vote by Writers," *The Philadelphia Inquirer*, Nov. 12, 1980, section Sports.

Wait Until '08? Think Again

"He's in scoring position...": Zolecki, Todd, "Howard getting a reputation," *The Philadelphia Inquirer*, Aug. 15, 2006, section Sports, C2.

A Mid-Summer Night's Dream

"When it comes to stealing the show...": Bostrom, Don, "Johnny Callison's Memorable Moment," The Morning Call, July 8, 1996, section Sports, C1.

"As it turned out, 1964 disintegrated...": Fernandez, Bernard, "A Greatest Hit: Callison's '64 HR," Philadelphia Daily News, July 14, 1987, section Sports, 80.

CHAPTER 5 – THE NUMBERS DON'T LIE
Number 500!

"I got my veteran, Robinson, out there...": Dolson, Frank, "Schmidt's Blast Was Better Than a Movie," *The Philadelphia Inquirer*, April 19, 1987, section Sports, F1.

"As soon as he hit it, there was no doubt...": Dolson, Frank and Stark, Jayson, "Schmidt's 500th Came Against a Worthy Opponent," *The Philadelphia Inquirer*, April 19, 1987, section Sports, F6.

"I could possibly be the last guy to ever do it...": Stark, Jayson, "A Staggering Feat," *The Philadelphia Inquirer*, April 19, 1987, section Sports, F2.

CHAPTER 6 – IT AIN'T OVER TILL IT'S OVER
1964

"During the 2007 season...": Chuck, Bill and Kaplan, Jim, *Walkoffs, Last Licks and Final Outs*, (Skokie, Illinois: ACTA Sports, 2008), p. 23-25.

CHAPTER 7 – THE DREAM TEAM: THE PLAYERS

"The 1880s were a time of extensive experimenting...": James,
Bill, *The New Bill James Historical Baseball Abstract* (New York:
Free Press, 2001), p. 35-37, 52-54.

Catcher
"A very smart receiver...": James, Bill, *The New Bill James
Historical Baseball Abstract* (New York: Free Press, 2001), p.
380, 391.

Second Base
"That's the first day...": Zolecki, Todd, "Utley gets boost from hit
movies," *The Philadelphia Inquirer*, July 24, 2007, section
Sports, D1.

"He spent hours as a kid at the Lakewood Batting Cages...":
Salisbury, Jim, "Utley riding high – just not on his old
skateboard," *The Philadelphia Inquirer*, July 11, 2006, section
Sports, C1.

Third Base
"I was totally lost mentally as a hitter...": Pascarelli, Peter,
"Schmidt Ends Two Slumps on One Blow – Home Run in
Ninth Lifts Phils," *The Philadelphia Inquirer*, May 29, 1983,
section Sports, D1.

Left Field
"This is the closest replica to Del I have ever seen...": James, Bill,
The New Bill James Historical Baseball Abstract, (New York:
Free Press, 2001), p. 658.

Right Field
"It was an easy target...": Westcott, Rich, *Philadelphia's Old
Ballparks* (Philadelphia: Temple University Press, 1996), p.
33-34.

CHAPTER 8 – THE DREAM TEAM: THE PITCHERS

Grover Cleveland Alexander

"His sinking fastball seemed fashioned from cement...": Kahn, Roger, *The Head Game* (Harcourt: New York, 2000), p. 305.

"See anything up there...": Westcott, Rich and Bilovsky, Frank, *The Phillies Encyclopedia* (Philadelphia: Temple University Press, 2004), p. 122-124.

Jim Bunning

"I remember we played a game in Montreal one time, in old Jarry Park...": Stark, Jayson, "At Last, A Place in Hall," *The Philadelphia Inquirer*, Aug. 4, 1996, section Sports, C1.

Curt Schilling

"If I get a hitter to swing at a 1-and-2 splitter...": Salisbury, Jim, "Schilling's Motto: Be Prepared," *The Philadelphia Inquirer*, April 21, 1998, section Sports, F1.

Tug McGraw

"At that time I started naming my pitches...": McGraw, Tug, *Ya Gotta Believe!* (New York: New American Library, 2004), p. 140.

"I was a hard-working guy...": Hofmann, Rich, "McGraw Still Will Have His Say In Philly," *Philadelphia Daily News*, Feb. 15, 1985, section Sports, 134.

CHAPTER 10 – THE MOVES THEY MADE

Fergie to the Cubs

"I never got the feeling from Mauch...": Ashburn, Rich, "Recalling Another Phils Throw-In: Ferguson Jenkins," *Philadelphia Daily News*, Aug, 20, 1985, section Sports, p. 81.

A Wise Move for Lefty

"I was like, in shock...": Dolson, Frank, "John Quinn's Deal? A Success After All," *The Philadelphia Inquirer*, Jan. 14, 1994, section Sports, C3.

"I think Carlton is the top pitcher in the National League...":
Dolson, Frank, "Getting Lefty the Right Move," *The
Philadelphia Inquirer*, Oct. 27, 1982, section Sports, D1.

Go Ahead, Take Sandberg

"We knew we had them over a barrel...": Dolson, Frank, "He Has
Proven the Phils Wrong," *The Philadelphia Inquirer*, Oct. 8,
1989, section Sports, E5.

"Sandberg is the biggest mistake we've made...": Conlin, Bill,
"Taste of Fine Ryne Rips Phils," *Philadelphia Daily News*, June
2, 1984, section Sports, 44.

"The Phillies drafted Sandberg in the 20th round in 1978...":
Ashburn, Rich, "Here's How Phils Evaluated Sandberg,"
Philadelphia Daily News, Nov. 15, 1984, section Sports, 99.

CHAPTER 11 – GREAT PERFORMANCES
Going Through an Art Museum on a Motorcycle

"There has never been a game like that one...": Fitzpatrick,
Frank, "Goodbye, Mr. McGraw," *The Philadelphia Inquirer*,
Jan. 7, 2004, section Sports, E1.

Happy Father's Day

"It didn't hit me until afterward...": Fitzpatrick, Frank, "An
Afternoon of Sheer Perfection," *The Philadelphia Inquirer*,
June 22, 1989, section Sports, D1.

"It was the only change up I had thrown in the whole game...":
Carchidi, Sam, "A magic Father's Day in '64," *The
Philadelphia Inquirer*, June 19, 2004, section Sports, D1.

We're Going Streaking!

"You're superstitious? ...": Zolecki, Todd, "A tale of two streaks:
Rollins, Utley handle pressure differently," *The Philadelphia
Inquirer*, Aug. 11, 2006, section Sports, C1.

Opposites Attract

"He comes to play every day...": Cushman, Tom, "No. 3,631 Was Special," *Philadelphia Daily News*, Aug. 11, 1981, section Sports, 67.

"Utley? I love that guy...": Salisbury, Jim, "Utley reveling in all things all-star," *The Philadelphia Inquirer*, July 16, 2008, section Sports, E1.

For Who? For What?

"We were playing no doubles...": Zolecki, Todd, "Phillies Report," *The Philadelphia Inquirer*, May 16, 2006, section Sports, F2.

CHAPTER 12 – OFF THE FIELD

The Phanatic

"Twenty-nine hundred and we own the copyright...": Giles, Bill, *Pouring Six Beers at a Time* (Chicago: Triumph Books, 2007), p. 113-116.

"I didn't know what to expect...": Ford, Bob, "Fantastic Phanatic," *The Philadelphia Inquirer*, July 26, 2002, section Sports, D1.